The Best of Secondary Assembly File

pfp

LONDON

First published in this format in 1998 by
pfp
61 Gray's Inn Road
London
WC1X 8TL.

Previously published in *The Secondary Assembly File* 1996–1997.

Printed in the UK.

ISBN 1 874050 39 2

A catalogue record for this book is available from the British Library.

CONTENTS

pfp, 61 Gray's Inn Road, London WC1X 8TL ISBN 1 874050 39 2

CONTENTS (CONTINUED)

pfp, 61 Gray's Inn Road, London WC1X 8TL May be photocopied for use within the purchasing institution only.
 ISBN 1 874050 39 2

INTRODUCTION

Welcome to The Best of Secondary Assembly File. This book is a compilation of assemblies taken from our highly successful Secondary Assembly File, which has been published in the form of three issues per year since 1996.

Selecting the best assemblies has been no easy task, but I hope that I have provided a good selection from the menu that will encourage you to return to try the rest of the feast. The themes that I have selected cover a wide range of key values such as 'Respect For The Rights Of Others' and 'Valuing Truth' as well as 'Respect For The Living Environment' and 'Having A Sense Of Personal Responsibility'. Nor have we been afraid to tackle some controversial topics – note the assembly on Abortion in the 'Choice And Decisions' theme and the assembly on AIDS in the 'Barriers' theme.

If you are new to The Secondary Assembly File you will find that all the assemblies can be taken off the shelf at short notice and read out in about 10 minutes, but that there is also room for extending and adapting them to your own school's needs and circumstances. As you will see, each assembly has a number of helpful features in it which have been put there in response to requests from some of our subscribers to The Secondary Assembly File.

There are five assemblies on each theme – one for each day of the week, should you wish to use that format. Each one begins with a short summary telling you what the assembly is about, and the key value that is dealt with in each theme is clearly identified. Each group of five assemblies includes a 'record slip' for you to use so that you and your colleagues know exactly when a particular assembly was taken, by whom and with which group of students. An OHT master is supplied for each theme, to help focus the students' attention on the issue being discussed. We also provide a list of any resources you might need.

As a Deputy Head Teacher myself I have to give many assemblies and I am always confident that if I pick up an assembly from The Secondary Assembly File it will challenge the students to think about moral and spiritual issues without being patronising. Multi-faith beliefs are a strong feature throughout and the themes give ample scope for schools to express their own values through the assemblies. Few of us have the ability to come up with stimulating and interesting ideas for assemblies two or three times a week and The Secondary Assembly File certainly helps me to maintain a high standard.

As I write this introduction, The Secondary Assembly File is going into its fourth year and continues to provide up-to-date assemblies with contemporary examples that maintain students' interest and give them the opportunity to reflect on moral and spiritual values. These values meet the demands of Ofsted when inspectors are looking to see whether or not a school meets the criteria for collective worship. They also form an important contribution to your school's efforts to produce good citizens for the future.

I hope you enjoy these assemblies and that using them successfully will encourage you to try The Secondary Assembly File in the future.

Larry Hartley
Series Editor
The Secondary Assembly File

The Secondary Assembly File – philosophy

What is the philosophy behind the Secondary Assembly File?

- To offer a framework around which people with a religious faith or none can unite with both honesty and integrity.
- To ensure an educational experience of the highest quality, which fulfils statutory requirements.
- To respect the family, cultural or religious background of all members of the school community.
- To promote the school's sense of community, offering experiences which are inclusive – enabling all members of the school to participate.
- To be consistent with the school's aims and philosophy and with the ideals and values pursued by the school.

The Secondary Assembly File helps to make explicit, and to celebrate, the agreed and shared values of a school as a part of the school's own strategy for the spiritual, moral, social and cultural development of students. It works within the shared attitudes, beliefs and values which the school has identified as the basis of its community and pastoral life. It is also seen as part of the means by which they will be realised within all aspects of school life.

What does the Secondary Assembly File offer?

The Secondary Assembly File offers a range of assemblies for collective worship based on inclusive themes. Each assembly or group of assemblies offers opportunities to nurture students in the shared values of the school and to reflect on more contentious areas of faith and belief. Each theme uses a framework which offers schools the means to produce affective experiences which express and celebrate their communal life and values; which reflect on events and issues – local, national or international; which develop awareness of questions of meaning and value in human life and which encourage positive responses.

One of the problems facing busy headteachers, heads of house, year leaders and others is the need to produce meaningful, relevant assemblies for collective worship within an already heavy schedule. A common problem is the lack of a structure or programme, which in turn leads to uncertainty, anxiety and the 'Sunday night dilemma'... *'What shall I do for assembly tomorrow?'*. The Secondary Assembly File suggests how suitable programmes might be developed.
Each theme is broken down into a sequence of assemblies for collective worship – each of which relates to elements of the framework shown below.

The opportunities for response are important for they leave open the possibility for ***affective*** experiences. The experiences listed in the following example highlight the type of responses which might be characteristic of school worship. It is a clear intention of the Secondary Assembly File to offer assemblies for collective worship which influence, change, impress and stir the members of the school community. Without opportunities for these affective responses, the assemblies for collective worship could not form part of the school's nurturing activity.

The Secondary Assembly File framework for school assemblies

Reflection
on a range of personal, social, moral or spiritual issues, which should be considered in a manner which is consistent with the agreed school values.

Response
to affirm and celebrate the agreed school values and to act in accordance with these; to encourage the students to aspire to higher values and visions of the good life; to encourage them to commit themselves to positive ways of living. As appropriate, this could be structured around five key responses:

1. celebration
2. acknowledging failures and shortcomings
3. expressions of thankfulness
4. commitment
5. action.

The following shows how **reflection** and **response** can be a focus for affective assemblies:

Opportunities to ***reflect*** on a range of personal, social, moral or spiritual issues in relation to the agreed school values, which might include the following:

- Reflect on the deeper aspirations of people. (How should the world be?)
- Reflect on the beliefs and values which motivate responsibly committed people.
- Reflect on the values which have shaped our cultural identity.
- Reflect on the ideas and questions which explore the 'Why?' of human behaviour, rather than merely the 'What?' or the 'How?'
- Reflect on the mystery of existence. (What is the purpose of life?)

Opportunities to ***respond*** in a manner which is in keeping with agreed school values. The students can be encouraged, but not coerced, to participate with the following key responses. They are free to respond or not, as the case may be.

Celebration

- Celebrate special occasions together, eg. birthdays, achievements.
- Celebrate achievement of various kinds, eg. spiritual, moral, cultural, mental, physical.
- Celebrate the diversity of faith, belief and commitment within the school community.

Acknowledging failures and shortcomings

- Recognise and respond to personal shortcomings, eg. selfishness, bullying, prejudice, carelessness about the environment, carelessness about their own education.
- Recognise and respond to society's shortcomings, eg. carelessness about the Third World, increase in crime (particularly amongst young people), social inequality.

Thankfulness

- Express thankfulness for the good things in life, eg. friends and family, comparative material prosperity, health, personal talents, music and the arts.

Commitment

- Reflect on their own commitments.
- Show concern for members of the school community.
- Express sympathy and compassion for the less fortunate within the world.
- Develop a sense of responsibility for, and stewardship of, the natural environment.
- Develop an admiration for, and commitment to, human qualities such as courage, honesty, sympathy and respect for others.
- Acknowledge the importance of commitment to positive beliefs and values.

Action

- Respond appropriately, as individuals, to examples of injustice, cruelty and exploitation.
- Support home and overseas charities.
- Respond with commitment to work hard and play hard.
- Support community projects, eg. local old people's home, local special school, nature conservancy projects, road safety projects.

Underpinning the Secondary Assembly File is a belief that assemblies for collective worship should allow teachers and students to come together to reflect on, affirm and celebrate shared values and aspirations. *Assemblies within the Secondary Assembly File help schools to make **explicit** the values which they wish to identify as the foundation for their activities and which are **implicit** in their community life and work, ie. 'This is the way we do things here'.*

Within assemblies for collective worship, the Secondary Assembly File helps teachers to develop the following two contrasting, yet compatible, emphases:

- The agreed or core beliefs and values which should be a source of reflection and could be promoted within the general life of the school.

- Those beliefs or values which are more contentious and which should not be promoted by the school as an institution. However, they might be a useful stimulus for reflection and discussion, particularly when they reflect the beliefs and values of faith groups within the school community. Their inclusion is consistent with attitudes and values such as 'respect for others', 'sharing' and a 'willingness to seek truth'.

Some other issues addressed within the Secondary Assembly File

The Secondary Assembly File starts from those values to which a school community is committed. It does not set out to indoctrinate into any particular set of beliefs.

This approach faces up to the reality of school populations which are increasingly plural- or multi-faith. It also recognises that real progress and development can be achieved only if there is a reasonable degree of consensus within a school. If many staff absent themselves from collective worship, what does this say to the students about the value of the gathering? In facing up to this reality, the Secondary Assembly File offers a way forward which will create a more positive response from a wider range of teachers.

Schools' concern with the spiritual aspects of life

'Spiritual' is not synonymous with 'religious'. The term 'spiritual' identifies those areas of experience which are at the heart of human motivation and responses to life. It is to do with the search for meaning and purpose in life; it concerns the deepest human qualities and values by which we live. It incorporates our responses to challenging experiences, eg. suffering, beauty and encounters with good and evil. For those with a religious faith, it also incorporates their encounter with the divine.

Many of the assemblies in the Secondary Assembly File are set within a context of 'nurture' or 'knowledge'; we believe this approach helps to clarify a school's responsibility for promoting the spiritual, moral, social and cultural development of students. These two strands run through all the assembly themes.

The first, *nurture*... describes the role of parents and carers, or of a school or some other institution, when they seek to foster in young people particular attitudes or a commitment to particular principles, beliefs or values. Family and school are the most important social groups for the very large majority of students. Each of these groups is expected to nurture children's attitudes, beliefs and values towards themselves, other people and the world around them. The fact that it is a shared responsibility does not mean that all those charged with the nurturing of children will do so on exactly the same basis.

A non-denominational school cannot be expected to nurture students in the beliefs and values of a particular religion. It would be wrong for one group to impose views, which are perceived to be contentious, on the remainder. To attempt to do so would show a lack of respect for others and amount to an infringement of individual rights.

The second, *knowledge*... is about beliefs and values, what they are and how they influence the lives of individuals and groups in society, etc. Learning beliefs and values will be found in many subjects, such as history, art, human geography, literature, music and health education. However, in RE, beliefs and values, ie. what beliefs and values are and how they influence human activity, are the main content of the subject. The range of beliefs and values which children learn about in RE and other subjects will normally be wider and more varied than the beliefs and values promoted within the school community.

The 'broadly Christian' nature of collective worship

There are two separate ways in which the 'broadly Christian' element can be identified and integrated into the collective act in a manner which is consistent with the philosophy of the Secondary Assembly File.

Looking for areas of common ground. There are numerous points of similarity between various religious faiths, as well as humanist perspectives. For example, some Christian moral values or ideas about the nature of forgiveness and reconciliation are similar to those of other faiths and philosophies. To develop an act of collective worship which focuses on such an issue could be broadly Christian, but it could also reflect the ideas and values of humanists, Jews, Muslims, etc. At an appropriate stage, senior students should be encouraged to understand that the root of such ideas and values may lie within fundamentally different beliefs.

A community – sharing experiences. It is important that students are aware of beliefs, ideas and values which may not be held by all those involved in the act of collective worship. Much depends in these instances upon the context within which such beliefs, ideas and values are introduced. Those leading school worship must be careful to avoid giving the impression that there is consensus about such beliefs or that students ought to accept them. For example, an act of worship at harvest time might initially explore 'What we can all be thankful for'. As a development of this idea, the students might listen to a specifically Christian reading which will begin with an introduction such as 'Christians believe that...' or 'Christians say that...'. Equally, this approach applies to the expression of the more specific beliefs and ideas of other faiths and philosophies.

Theme

Haves and have-nots

Assemblies on this theme

1 **Metamorphosis**
This assembly encourages students to enter into the experience of Developing World poverty in order to appreciate the difference between necessities and luxuries.

2 **Well, what can I do about it?**
This assembly encourages students to acknowledge their own role in making the changes that give people in the Developing World new hope.

3 **Donkeys, driers and watermills**
This assembly describes some relatively simple projects, appropriate to the Developing World, which improve rural people's chances of staying on the land, reducing urban migration and subsequent poverty. Students are encouraged to appreciate the difference between hand-outs and appropriate self-help support.

4 **Have you no home to go to?**
This assembly challenges students to show compassion and understanding for those who are homeless.

5 **These streets aren't paved with gold**
This assembly uses the traditional parable of the Prodigal Son to introduce some thoughts about why people leave home and to examine our reactions to homeless people.

Record of use

Taken by	1	2	3	4	5
Date					
Given to					

Comments

pfp, 61 Gray's Inn Road, London WC1X 8TL May be photocopied for use within the purchasing institution only.
 ISBN 1 874050 39 2

Theme/ Key value

Haves and have-nots

Respect for the rights of others

Title

Metamorphosis

Summary

This assembly encourages students to think about the experience of Developing World poverty and to appreciate the difference between necessities and luxuries.

Resources

Nothing at all.

REFLECTION

Some of the world's most exciting stories are the ones that tell of a spectacular transformation. You know – the frog that turns into a prince, the ugly duckling who grows up to be a swan, Cinderella becoming a princess and Clarke Kent becoming Superman.

Or perhaps you think these stories are a bit on the tame side. You prefer the more sinister stories where the transformation goes in the other direction – where Dr Jekyll becomes Mr Hyde or Count Dracula turns into a vampire. Perhaps you like the film *Interview with a Vampire*, where Tom Cruise persuades people to become vampires.

Whichever way the transformation goes, the word for that kind of complete change of character and appearance is metamorphosis.

Sometimes it's fun to daydream about metamorphosis, about changing into somebody else – perhaps a person in a story, or in a film or on television. It's fun to dream, so long as the metamorphosis is in the right direction. But what if you were watching a TV news item or documentary about a poor, undernourished child picking over a rubbish dump on the edge of a South American city, and you suddenly found yourself transformed, and you were that child? How would you feel then?

It's hard to imagine living in the Developing World. Here in our comfortable Developed World we have very little experience of the kind of poverty and despair that puts people on the rubbish dump – quite literally.

Here's one way to imagine how it would feel to live in the Developing World. Imagine your home as it is now. You can start transforming it into a Developing World home by removing a few things in your mind – the beds, the sofas, tables, chairs, cupboards, TV, computer, all the clothes you're not wearing right now, all the kitchen equipment, pretty well all the food, the taps, the sink, the bath, the loo, all the electricity. In fact, get rid of the whole house (or flat/apartment) and move your family into a small garden shed. Give them a few blankets, a table, one wooden chair. For yourself you can have your oldest tattiest set of clothes, but no shoes. Your dad can have a pair of old shoes, but no one else. You can have £2 in savings between all of you, plus a small bag of flour, a little sugar and some salt.

Your mum is desperate for more food to make a meal for the family. She reckons you might find an old chicken carcass or some thrown-out cold potatoes on the local rubbish dump... *(Pause)*

OK. You can come back now.

Fortunately, we only have to imagine living like that. But for millions of people in Developing World countries, that kind of destitution is the only life they know. For them, there's no way of escape. All they can do is imagine what it would be like to be adequately fed and clothed and living in a home with real beds and clean water. Anything more than that would be luxury beyond their wildest dreams... things like milk in the fridge, two sets of clothes, clean bedding, soap, toothpaste. Things we'd call necessities.

If you found yourself metamorphosed into a citizen of a Developing World country, what would you miss the most from your Developed World existence? Just think of some of the things – objects – around your home that you'd miss if you didn't have them with you. The TV perhaps, the video, your wall posters, your CDs, your collection of special bits and pieces, the family pet, or even the family car. Now think of what else you'd miss – having space and time to do things with your friends – whether it's doing a play, or playing football, or watching a video or just messing around. Having the freedom to visit different places or to go on holiday. And what about those things you think of as necessities – the loo, the phone, your bed, your own toothbrush?

We wouldn't consider any of these things as luxuries. Most of them aren't even absolute necessities. We could live without them. But of course we wouldn't want to.

Tomorrow (later in the week) we'll be considering some of the things that cause the big gap between life in the Developed World and life in the Developing World. And we'll be thinking about ways that could change the situation. But for today, we've one more transformation to make. Instead of considering ways we can help the people of the Developing World, we're going to work a very particular metamorphosis. Instead of thinking of us as 'the ones who give' and them as 'the ones who receive', let's turn the tables and think about what the citizens of the Developing World give to us.

They don't directly give us food (although we sometimes buy food from them), or money or medical aid. What they do give us is some idea of what the absolute necessities of life really are. Warmth, nourishment, clothing, water. Things every human being ought to be able to take for granted. If we have more than these basic necessities, we are very lucky indeed. And if it takes an image of a child picking over a rubbish dump to show us how lucky we are, then we should acknowledge our thanks for what that child has given us.

RESPONSE

Expressions of thankfulness

In a moment of quiet, let us all think about the basic necessities of life – clean water, sufficient food, warm clothes, our own shoes. Are we grateful that we have these things? Or do we just take them for granted? *(Pause)*

Now, let us think of those special things we'd miss if they weren't there as part of our lives – the things, the objects, we'd miss. *(Pause)* The activities we'd miss. *(Pause)* The ordinary necessities we'd miss, like the phone or the loo. *(Pause)* Are we grateful for these things? Or do we just take them for granted?

Finally, let us acknowledge our thankfulness for all these things that we have and others don't have. You might consider saying an actual thank you to someone at home later, if that's appropriate. But just now, in the silence, you could admit that you are thankful that you live in the Developed World and perhaps commit yourself to playing your part in bridging the gap between the Developed World and the Developing World. If you believe in God, you may wish to express these thoughts to Him. *(Pause)*

Extra Resources

There is a wide range of resources to support this theme. We have made just a few suggestions for materials which link particularly well with a specific assembly. Various film versions of Dr Jekyll – you could show the extract where Jekyll changes into Hyde.

Jenkins, S (1993) *A World Of Difference*. Oxford: Lion Publishing plc.

pfp, 61 Gray's Inn Road, London WC1X 8TL ISBN 1 874050 39 2

Theme/ Key value

Haves and have-nots

Respect for the rights of others

Title

Well, what can I do about it?

Summary

This assembly encourages students to acknowledge their own role in making the changes that give people in the Developing World new hope.

Resources

9 students to read parts of the Reflection section. Supplied OHT image (p12).
Optional 9 narrow boxes with a key term written on each: Malnutrition; Illness; Large families; Population growth; Poverty; Urban migration; Shortage of shelter and food; Malnutrition (again). Put them in a line on a table like dominoes, close enough so that they will hit each other when they fall. Each of the 9 students should stand behind a box.

REFLECTION

In some parts of the world, adults and children pick over the rubbish on the local tip looking for food or for something to sell. Imagine having to rely on a rubbish tip for your day-to-day survival! It makes you wonder how people get to be that poor. There are several factors that cause this kind of poverty in the Developing World, and they're like a chain reaction – one leads to another.

- ***Optional*** *The 9 students read their passages in turn. They should hold up each box as they do so, so that the key words can be seen, and then put them back in exactly the same spot.*

Box 1 Shortage of food and poor diet causes malnutrition.

Box 2 Malnutrition plus dirty water and poor sanitation cause illness and disease.

Box 3 Bad health affects children most. Many children die before their fifth birthday.

Box 4 Because children die, parents try to have large families to make sure there is someone to look after them in their old age and to help them with work.

Box 5 Large families producing more large families means rapid population growth.

Box 6 Large families can lead to poverty in country areas, as more and more people try to live off the same section of land.

Box 7 When the land will no longer support them, the country people uproot and go to live in the towns. This is known as 'urban migration'. Life in the city seems more attractive and perhaps better quality.

Box 8 There isn't enough work or places to live in the towns for all the new arrivals and there's no unemployment benefit. So people have to rely on help from relatives, or finding odd jobs, or recycling rubbish, or begging. This means the people don't have much money.

Box 9 Most of a Developing World person's income is spent on food. So low income means less food. Shortage of food and bad diet causes malnutrition.

- *Push the first box so that it falls into the next and they all fall over, like dominoes.*

And that's where we started, of course – food shortage, malnutrition, disease, children dying, large families, not enough land in the countryside, not enough jobs in the town, low income, food shortage, and so on and so on.

People living inside that kind of vicious circle can become very fatalistic. After a while it's easy for them to believe that nothing can be done to change their situation, and to lose all sense of hope of a better kind of life in the future.

In 1984, singer Bob Geldof saw this effect when he became the organiser of Band

Aid and Live Aid and visited famine-stricken Ethiopia. He said afterwards, 'It was not the physical affliction that most upset me, though that was bad enough... What was worse than all that was the look in their eyes. They were glazed, blank and vacuous. They looked but did not see. They were the eyes of people who had given up.'

Of course, in times of famine, the thing people need is food. But to smash the poverty chain, to break that awful vicious circle, these people need more than food, or tents, or medicine – what we call 'emergency aid'. These things stop people dying in the short term but they don't change their lives.

These people need hope. And they can only start to hope when they see evidence that change is possible. Think back to that Developing World poverty chain. Some things can be changed, with a little help from the Developed World. Disease can be controlled by helping people to install wells and pumps to supply clean water. Land can be improved – perhaps by drainage ditches or by irrigation channels – to produce larger and better crops.

Then there wouldn't be the same need to move into the cities. This kind of help is called development work. Emergency aid stops people dying, but development work helps them to improve their own situation. It gives them hope for a better kind of life in the future.

There's what's called a 'Development way' of helping to bring about change, and that's by making sure that poor countries are not treated unfairly by rich countries when it comes to trading on the world markets. If you had sugar on your cereal this morning, do you know whether it was produced from European sugar beet, or from sugar-cane grown in the Developing World? The European Community produces far more sugar than it needs, then sells it cheaply around the world. This forces the price down and reduces possible income for Developing World sugar-cane growers.

Many countries are at a disadvantage like this because the West controls and dominates world trade. Trade reform is slowly being brought about by ordinary people in the Developed World – persuading politicians and trading companies to treat Developing World countries more fairly.

RESPONSE

Action

- *Show the supplied OHT image of the child on the rubbish tip.*

You look at a picture like that and you think, 'Well, what can I do?' For a start, let us just think quietly of those links in the Developing World poverty chain – malnutrition, disease, population growth, poor land, urban migration, unemployment, malnutrition, disease... *(Pause)* Think of some of the food we enjoy from Developing World countries – things we take for granted, like sugar, tea, coffee, cocoa. Perhaps we ought to wonder more often whether the growers got a fair deal or not.

We can be thankful for the charities that help with development work. Perhaps you can think about ways of supporting them like buying products with the Fair Trade symbol on them or giving regularly, which allows for forward planning. *(Pause)* Whether it's Emergency Aid, Development Work or Trade Reform, there are many things we can do to help get that child off that rubbish tip.

Leave the image showing as the students leave in the usual way

Extra Resources

Charities and organisations who will help with resources and information are: Action Aid 01460 62972, Cafod 0171 7337900, CARE 0171 379 5247, Christian Aid 0171 6204444, Oxfam 01865 312603, Save the Children Fund 0171 7035400, SOS Sahel 0171 8379129, UNICEF 0171 4055592. Some will provide speakers for PSE/tutor groups or assemblies. Telephone numbers are correct at time of publication.

Theme/ Key value

Haves and have-nots

Respect for the rights of others

Title

Donkeys, driers and watermills

Summary

This assembly describes some relatively simple projects, appropriate to the Developing World, which improve rural people's chances of staying on the land, reducing urban migration and subsequent poverty. Students are encouraged to appreciate the difference between hand-outs and appropriate self-help support.

Resources

Supplied OHT image (p12).

REFLECTION

In many Developing World countries, people fall into the poverty pit when their land won't support them and they migrate to the nearest city in the hope of finding a job. Too often, as we have seen, they finish up on the rubbish tip – quite literally.

If only the land could support more people, that would be one way of ending this kind of poverty. But one problem is that if you're growing crops not just to eat, but also to sell so that you can buy things like clothes and tools, you've got to get your crops to market. And in some parts of the world, the only way to do that is to physically pick up your bundles of crops and carry them. Rural people spend a lot of time and effort just carrying things – water, wood and crops.

Now it would be no help at all to raise funds here at school and send them a big container lorry. Or even a little pick-up truck. Hand-outs like that would be insulting, because these people have no access to decent roads, fuel, motor maintenance or parts. (And it would add to pollution.)

But a couple of donkeys… that would be a different matter. One development agency is currently introducing the donkey to parts of Africa that have not known it before. The results are quite dramatic. Donkeys are easy to train, easy to feed, willing to work and versatile. With a simple humane harness they can pull a plough or a cart, or carry a pack, leaving their owners more time and energy to spend tending and extending their crops.

Some Developing World farmers wanting to sell crops are a long distance from the nearest markets. Too far even for a donkey cart. A little lateral thinking has come up with an ideal solution for these growers.

Herbs, flowers, fruit, cashew nuts and some vegetables can all be sold dried as well as fresh. Some farmers in Peru, in South America, are now using tray-driers to dry their crops. A tray-drier is like a huge airing cupboard, where warm air is forced through the trays to dry the crops. The dried goods can then be stored without losing their quality until they can be delivered or collected.

But perhaps the greatest help to rural communities is access to electricity. Motor-power increases any farm's efficiency, whether it's for operating tray-driers, or water-pumps, or basic lighting. Some people are using rechargeable batteries, but the journey to the nearest recharging centre can be long and arduous.

Here's where one of the oldest technologies in the world comes into its own. High in the Andes mountains, water-powered stone mills, which have milled grain for local farmers for 500 years, are now being improved and adapted to charge batteries as well.

Donkeys, driers and watermills. They don't mean much to people like us who have become dependent on motorways, food-processing plants and power stations. But in some parts of the world, donkeys, driers and watermills are making life possible for rural communities. Not just possible, but profitable. Which means that people are not tempted to head for the city and the rubbish tip.

RESPONSE

Expressions of thankfulness

Thank goodness our lives don't depend on what we grow ourselves. *(If your school has a healthy eating policy you could substitute vegetables and fruit juice for coke and crisps in this next sentence.)* We're so used to buying our crisps and coke from the shop, or unloading superstore bags from the boot of the car, that we forget there are people in the world who eat only what they grow. And most of the time we don't care if their land isn't supporting them. *(Pause)*

- *Show the supplied image of child on the rubbish tip.*

Thank goodness that could never be a picture of someone from this school. A picture like that should make us very thankful for our homes, our food, our health, our future. *(Pause)* You might want to express your thanks in a silent prayer. *(Pause)* And think for a moment about people who have to live like that. *(Pause)*

> ***Optional*** *You could encourage groups and/or individuals to take some positive action and support a Developing World Action project; here are some words you can adapt to your own context:*
>
> *Some groups/classes are/could be involved in supporting charities and aid agencies. But there's nothing to stop individuals getting in touch with these organisations, too. Your tutor/year leader can get information for you. There are hundreds of projects needing help out there, not just donkeys, driers and watermills.)*

Extra Resources

Intermediate Technology (May 1993) Current Mini Projects in Need of Funding.
There are a number of charities and organisations who will help with resources and information, usually at a reasonable cost.
Here are some suggestions: Action Aid 01460 62972, Cafod 0171 7337900, CARE 0171 379 5247, Christian Aid 0171 6204444, Oxfam 01865 312603, Save the Children Fund 0171 7035400, SOS Sahel 0171 8379129, UNICEF 0171 4055592. Some will provide speakers for PSE/tutor groups or assemblies.

Theme/ Key value

Haves and have-nots

Respect for the rights of others

Title

Have you no home to go to?

Summary

This assembly challenges students to show compassion and understanding for those who are homeless.

Resources

Bible reading – *Matthew* 25 verses 37 to 40. Accurate figures relating to your own school population, ie. how may times does it go into 156 000? (See paragraph 9)
Optional A prepared OHT showing the figures in paragraph 9 below.

REFLECTION

When you crashed out of bed this morning, falling over the radio, the unfed cat and a pile of your dirty washing... Or, if you're wonderful, when you crashed out of bed this morning getting the milk off the doorstep, making your mum a cup of tea and putting the rubbish in the dustbin... Whatever way you started the day, you almost certainly took 'home' for granted.

For most of us, home is more than just a roof over our heads. Having a safe and familiar home-base gives a person a sense of identity, a feeling of security and the confidence and personal dignity to cope with the world outside. So being homeless robs you of more than just your roof.

When your parents were young, people used to associate homelessness and begging with the cities of underdeveloped foreign countries. You saw very little begging on the streets of Britain or other Western countries. You might have seen an occasional tramp or bag-lady sleeping on a park bench, but you never saw teenagers sleeping rough in shop doorways or in makeshift cardboard shelters. People used to think that homelessness on a wide scale couldn't happen in an advanced economic society like ours.

But now we encounter homeless people on the streets of most of our towns, and – if we're honest – we often find it difficult to know how to respond. You hear the plea, 'Got a bit of spare change for a cup of tea, please?' You wonder how on earth a homeless person can manage to own a dog on a string. Or you walk through a subway and you see someone ill and undernourished, huddled in a corner with a roughly made sign – 'homeless and hungry, please help'. The message is always the same. It always seems to say 'You've got something, I've got nothing – what are you going to do about it?' And you probably struggle with mixed emotions.

You feel pity for anyone who hasn't got a home. You feel guilty about your own home comforts. You feel indignant – why doesn't this person get a proper job? You feel suspicious because you've read in the papers about buskers who earn hundreds of pounds a week. You feel intimidated by someone who dares you to walk past without dropping money at their feet.

Homelessness is not just a problem for the homeless. It's a problem for all of us.

Optional *Show your prepared OHT.*

There are about 156 000 young people under the age of 25 who are homeless in Britain each year. We're talking about *(insert the figure for your school here)* times the population of our school with no evening meal tonight and all looking for a corner to doss down in.

So where did they all come from, these homeless young people? Well, more than 40% of them have been in local authority care as children. But local authority care stops at age 16 and then the state is no

© pfp 1998 ISBN 1 874050 39 2

longer responsible. So every week, up and down the country, there are 16-year-olds being told, 'Here's your things, here's a few pounds – off you go!' And it's not easy to claim benefit if you're between 16 and 18 years old, especially if you've nowhere to live. So although many go on to have successful and happy lives, there are a few for whom things are very difficult.

Others leave their family home when relationships get so sour that there seems to be no alternative. If you feel you're not wanted by your parents, if you're perhaps being knocked about by the adults at home, it takes a lot of courage to talk about your problems to someone else, like a teacher or a youth leader or a social worker. It sometimes seems a whole lot simpler just to grab your things and clear off. And anyway, you don't always have the choice. Some young people are thrown out of the family home at 16.

Dean knows what it's like to be homeless. He was brought up in foster homes and children's homes and joined the army at 16. But a knee injury saw him invalided out before he was 18. He had a nervous breakdown and spent some time in a psychiatric hospital. After that there was nowhere to go but the streets, as he moved from one town to another trying to get a job. But employers needed a proper address. It's a vicious circle.

Dean says, 'The general public slag off homeless people because they don't understand them. You can't live on the streets, under a hedge or whatever and then get up and go to work! It's just impossible. To get a job, you need clean clothes, you need to be mentally sound. You need to be able to get up, get on public transport and be accepted by ordinary people. A homeless person can't do that – you have to get through one day at a time, keep warm, get money for food.'

Dean survived, but many don't. Eight of the homeless people that Dean met on the streets committed suicide. Homeless people are 34 times more likely to commit suicide than those with a home-base.

Survival isn't easy. Dean recalls, 'I survived by feeding myself out of skips and rubbish bins. I did a bit of begging. Clothes came and went – one week you'd be well togged out, then someone would nick everything except what you were wearing. Also,' he says, 'I've always believed that I could cope with anything – my best foster home started me on that – and as I get older it gets more important. That belief definitely helped me survive when I was really low but sometimes it's hard to hold on to it.'

Dean now lives in a council flat in Cambridge. 'If I became homeless again,' he says, 'I think I'd kill myself. I just couldn't go through it all again. I pray to God it'll never happen.'

RESPONSE

Expressions of thankfulness

The Christian Bible records the words of Jesus on this matter. He said that people who just talk about the poor and do nothing are not his followers. Some of you may not share the Christian faith but his sentiment is one which we can all consider – that actions often do speak louder than words.

- ***Optional*** *Read Matthew 25 verses 37 to 40.*

A stable home gives a person a sense of identity, security and the confidence and personal dignity to cope with the world outside. You might like to think or pray about your home. Perhaps you want to express your gratitude for what you take for granted. *(Pause)* Maybe you need to find the courage to talk to someone about a problem. *(Pause)* As we think of young people like Dean, we can all resolve to show more care and understanding for people who are homeless.

Extra Resources

'A fair day's fiddle', Roger McGough (1987) *Melting into the Foreground*, Penguin.

Publicity pack from Shelter (1991) *No Fixed Abode*.

Theme/ Key value

Haves and have-nots

Respect for the rights of others

Title

These streets aren't paved with gold

Summary

This assembly uses the traditional parable of the Prodigal Son to introduce some thoughts about why people leave home and to examine our reactions to homeless people.

Resources

Three students to read the story. Photocopies of the relevant part of the assembly as a script.

REFLECTION

If you've ever wished you could leave home, you're expressing a desire that millions of young people have experienced right through history. Today, you might think about finding a flat – perhaps with a friend – and getting a job to pay the rent. And after that, it's up to you what you do, what you wear, where you go and who you go with. Independence. It sounds great, doesn't it?

Two thousand years ago, Jesus told a story about a son who couldn't wait to leave home.

■ *Here hand over the assembly to three students to read the parts of the younger son, father and the narrator.*

Narrator There was once a man who had two sons. The younger one said to him:

Younger son I'm leaving home. I want to lead a different life than this. I know when you die I'll inherit my share of your wealth but I want it now.

Narrator After some time – and with reluctance – the man divided some of his property between his two sons. After a few days the younger son sold his share and left home with the money. He went to a country far away. He thoroughly enjoyed himself. He spent everything he had. He spent it quickly. To put it mildly, he was reckless.

Then a severe famine spread over that country. The younger son had no money left and food was scarce. So he got a job looking after pigs. He ate very little and earned even less. He found himself wanting to eat the bean pods the pigs ate, he was so hungry. At last he came to his senses.

Younger son Back home, my father's hired workers have more than they can eat, and here I am about to starve! I've been crazy. I'll go back home to my father and apologise. I'll tell him that I've sinned against God and I'm no longer fit to be called his son. I don't expect him to respect me but if he at least takes me on as one of his hired workers, I'll be grateful.

Narrator So the younger son got up and started back to his father. *(Pause)* He was still a some distance away from home when his father saw him. His heart was filled with pity and joy, and he ran, threw his arms around his son, and kissed him. The son said:

Younger son Father, I 've sinned against God and against you. I am no longer fit to be called your son.

Narrator But the father called his servants:

Father Hurry! Bring the best robe and put it on him. Put a ring on his finger and shoes on his feet. Then go and get the prize calf and kill it, and let's celebrate with a feast! For this son of mine was dead, but now he's alive; he was lost, but now he 's been found.

Narrator And so the feasting began.

© pfp 1998 ISBN 1 874050 39 2

This is quite a difficult story to understand. The father forgave his son because he had seen the error of his ways. But to put the best robe on him? What about the other son who had always known the more sensible thing to do? Did he get rewarded too?

And what does the story tell us about people who leave home? Perhaps it tells us that there is no need to take personal responsibility for anything – that we will always be forgiven. After all, the son wasted his money, came home and was treated royally. Can this be what the story means?

Does this story have any relevance to people who leave home today?

Certainly there are young people who leave home from all sorts of different backgrounds, wealthy and poor. Not everyone suffers or becomes homeless. Many make a perfectly good start to the rest of their lives.

For those who don't, some can return home, take stock and start again. But many find that much more difficult. Perhaps their parents don't have much money and are unable to support them any more. Perhaps the bad feeling which caused them to leave home in the first place makes it too difficult for them to return.

The father in the story I read to you must have been heartbroken when his son left home. Heartbroken, angry, worried and confused. Wealthy or not, the longer his son stayed away the stronger these feelings must have grown. But in the end, the one thing he was able to do was accept his son back as he was.

Some homeless people are homeless by choice of a sort – even if life is difficult for them, it may be the better option. Others are homeless through no fault or choice of their own. The question we need to ask is – who will accept the homeless as they are? Who will step in and act as the parent when there is no parent actually able to do that? Who will provide the support that they need?

Homeless people need understanding and tolerance from society – that's us – and a realistic and compassionate housing policy from the authorities. Sure, there will be those who abuse it but there will be many more who will deeply grateful. It's only when you are sleeping on the streets that you realise they are not paved with gold.

RESPONSE

Expressions of thankfulness

Just think about where you'll sleep tonight. Whether you live in a big house or a small flat, it's better than a shop doorway. *(Pause)*

Sometimes it's difficult to understand and sympathise with homeless people. It's easy to think it's their own fault if they're lonely or ill or abused. Perhaps they shouldn't have left home. But perhaps they would have suffered worse abuse if they'd stayed. *(Pause)*

In the story Jesus told, the father could have said 'On your bike!' when the son came back. Perhaps the father's love and welcome are an example for us to follow. *(Pause)*

Jesus once said, 'Foxes have holes, and birds have nests, but the Son of Man has nowhere to lay down and rest.' (*Matthew* 8 verse 20) *(Pause)* Jesus identified with the homeless.

Extra Resources

Publicity pack from Shelter (1991) *No Fixed Abode*. Bible reading, *Luke* 15 verses 11 to 27.

Ed. Perry, M (1989) *Dramatised Bible*. London: Marshall Pickering/Bible Society.

 ISBN 1 874050 39 2

Theme

Bullying

Assemblies on this theme

1 No problem here
This assembly introduces the week's theme, which sets out to promote the core value of respect for others by exploring the topic of bullying.

2 Jealousy
This assembly considers how jealousy might be a cause of bullying. There is Part 2 of the story about Rajinder (Part 1 was in Assembly 1) and the story of Joseph and his coat of many colours.

3 It's not your fault
Some bullied children believe that the problem lies with them – that bullying will stop if the victim changes the way he or she is. This assembly reinforces the view that it is the school's responsibility to protect its students from bullying, and that the school does not expect victims to shoulder the responsibility by changing their behaviour.

4 Get you after school
The baggage which the phrase 'Get you after school' carries with it brings worry to students and parents and continual concern to heads and teachers. The threat itself can cause distress and disruption, even if there is no intent to carry it out. This assembly addresses some of these issues and invites students to reflect on effective ways of resolving conflict. It also raises the issue of the rights of others, which is treated as a separate theme in Secondary Assembly File.

5 Do they like doing it?
The evidence is that bullies do not 'delight' in making other people miserable. In fact, the inner feelings of bully and bullied are remarkably similar, and essentially have to do with lack of self-esteem – or self confidence if you prefer the term. This assembly uses this principle in an attempt to get bullies to reflect on how they might feel better if they tried other kinds of relationships.

Record of use

	1	2	3	4	5
Taken by					
Date					
Given to					

Comments

 ISBN 1 874050 39 2

BULLYING • OHT

Theme/ Key value

Bullying

Respect for others

Title

No problem here

Summary

This assembly introduces the week's theme, which sets out to promote the core value of respect for others by exploring the topic of bullying.

Resources

The supplied OHT image (p24) for this week can be used as and when you think fit.

REFLECTION

Every now and again bullying hits the national news. Sometimes it's because there has been a tragedy – a student has committed suicide, or attempted to. We see anguished parents and relatives being interviewed, and telling us how the young victim was distressed, and perhaps how the school had not been able to stop the problem. Or perhaps bullying is in the news because there's been yet another report, or a scheme to try to stop bullying.

Bullying makes news, I suspect, because the people who report the news – reporters, television presenters – all know exactly what it is. Perhaps they were bullied at school. Perhaps, even, they were bullies and are now inwardly ashamed. Perhaps their own children are bullied. Almost everyone, children and adults, has experience of it, and they know it's serious and so they take it seriously.

This school is against bullying. We tell your parents so. We have an anti-bullying policy. We work hard to protect you all against being intimidated or attacked by other students. Do we always succeed? You know the answer to that better than I do. You know whether you are still bullied, despite all the efforts of your teachers, your parents and your good friends. And you also know whether you still get away with bullying, despite all our efforts.

Part of the problem is that although bullying is always intimidation of one person by another – or by a group of people – this intimidation comes in different forms.

Think of what bullying can be. It can be a gang waiting on the way home to 'get' someone they have taken a dislike to.

It can be a number of people constantly interfering with one person's property – hiding shoes and books, spoiling work.

It can be a group of people deliberately shutting one person out of conversation and friendship.

It can also be – and I know many of you realise this – something very subtle and yet very cruel. Let me tell you just a very short story.

Rajinder sat in the second row by the window. The desk beside her was empty, because when the class came into the room nobody had tried to sit there. In fact several of the other girls quite deliberately walked past and sniffed or turned their noses up to emphasise the fact that they were definitely not going to sit there.

Rajinder glanced to one side. Across the room, Naomi caught her eye for a moment, and then deliberately smirked and leaned across to Melanie. For a moment their heads were together, and then they drew apart and laughed loudly, and Naomi glanced once again at Rajinder with that smirk on her face.

Behind Melanie, Rachel picked up the cue. She too glanced at Rajinder, then she quickly wrote something on a piece of paper and passed it forward. Melanie looked at it and then burst out again in a peal of laughter. And this time all three girls glanced across at Rajinder as their laughter subsided to a snigger.

Miss Ratcliffe walked in at that moment. 'Well, you three. What's the joke?'

'Nothing Miss,' said Melanie in that bright and friendly voice that made her so popular with her teachers.

Rajinder turned to look out of the window, to avoid the last triumphant glance that she knew would be coming from her three tormentors. She felt desperately unhappy – and the feeling wasn't helped by the fact that she wasn't sleeping very well. A tear formed and she hurriedly wiped it away with thc back of her hand.

Optional *Discussion – either now if the group is small enough, or simply leave the questions for personal reflection.*

Let me ask you one or two things:

Is Rajinder being bullied?

I know the answer to that. I know that for every incident of violent bullying, there are a dozen examples of the kind of unkindness that Rajinder suffers.

Does it hurt her? How does it hurt her? Could that happen in our school? Does that happen in our school?

How can we, in our school, today, stop that kind of thing from happening?

Should Melanie and the others be punished? What would they be punished for?

Could they perhaps be brought together with Rajinder so that Rajinder could tell them her own feelings? Would that help?

RESPONSE

Acknowledging failures and shortcomings

Let's face it, we all, if we're honest, take some pleasure from the distress of other people. *(Pause)* In Germany they have a special word for this feeling – *Schadenfreude*. It feels especially strong when the person in distress seems to deserve it.

But the trouble is, we can kid ourselves that the person deserves it when it's really us that wants to be unkind to them.

And worst of all, we can just pick on somebody for the sake of it, without thinking of the effect on the person we pick on.

So let's try and change things.

Action

Today – this day, starting now. Every time we feel like being unpleasant to someone, we'll just stop and think how it might feel to be on the receiving end. We're not going to turn into angels. We're just going to think how we affect other people.

Extra Resources

There is a wide range of publications associated with bullying.
Elliott, Michelle *Teenage Training Pack*. Available from Kidscape, World Trade Centre, Europe House, 3rd Floor, London E1 9AA.
For materials related to school and staff development, *Bullying: Schools do make a difference* published by Essex County Council Education Department (ISBN 0904 428 095) gives an excellent overview. There's also some useful poetry such as *Four O'Clock Friday* by John Foster, *Bully For You* by Ian Souter and *Bully Asleep* by John Walsh, all of which have been anthologised.

Theme/ Key value

Bullying

Respect for others

Title

Jealousy

Summary

This assembly considers how jealousy might be a cause of bullying. It contains Part 2 of Rajinder's story (Part 1 was in Assembly 1) and the story of Joseph and his coat of many colours.

Resources

Optional Five readers for the Joseph story. A quote from your school's mission statement referring to the value of every student.

REFLECTION

'Jealous! Me? Why would I be jealous of her/him of all people?' Have you ever said that? If you're honest, you probably have been jealous, even if you said you weren't. Jealousy is a powerful and destructive feeling. Consider for a moment what jealousy is...

Jealousy comes when you are convinced that someone is in a better position than you are, and you cannot accept it and be comfortable with it. You might display your jealousy in lots of different ways – trying to undermine the other person, being aggressive to them, talking about them vindictively, unfairly discriminating against them. And if you are stronger or more aggressive than the person you are jealous of, then before you know where you are you've become a bully. By doing this you have shown that you are not at ease with yourself. You're not comfortable with what you are. And that's a shame, because every major religion tells us that God accepts us as we are, unconditionally.

Our school believes that every student is valuable to us. Every one of you is worth our concern and attention.

- *Refer to school mission statement, prospectus, message on the letter heading, or whatever is appropriate here.*

What does jealousy do to the jealous person? What does it do to the person who is the target? Listen to this short story. It picks up from where yesterday's *(or the previous)* assembly left off...

Melanie was good at her work. She didn't feel happy, though. For one thing there was this business with Rajinder. There was just something about Rajinder that made her annoyed. It was difficult to know what it really was. Rajinder was a good-looking girl, quiet, and always neat in her school uniform. She wasn't interested in bands or football teams. Melanie thought that was strange, but when she asked Rajinder about it she didn't seem at all bothered.

Melanie couldn't accept that. For Melanie, which bands you liked and your favourite music and team were very important. It didn't seen natural not to be bothered. And yet she had an uneasy feeling that Rajinder really didn't care about such things, and that she had a perfectly good life without them.

But she wasn't jealous of Rajinder! She pulled a face at the thought. One of the other girls in the class had accused her of that. 'The trouble with you three (that meant Melanie and Naomi and Rachel) is that you're jealous of Rajinder because she's so calm and together,' she'd said.

'Calm and together, is it!' Melanie had thought. 'She'll not be so calm when we've finished having a go at her.' And so every day now, the three of them would find a way of getting at Rajinder. They would just look at her most of the time, and make comments together, and laugh. Melanie had a feeling it was going to get worse. Naomi was looking at Rajinder's locker this morning, and wondering whether she could open it with a key she had at home.

If they could get into Rajinder's locker, thought Melanie, they could do... Oh they could do all sorts of things. That would be

pfp, 61 Gray's Inn Road, London WC1X 8TL May be photocopied for use within the purchasing institution only.

good fun. But – was fun the right word? Melanie felt quite confused about that.

The Bible has several things to say about jealousy. In fact each of the major religions understands how destructive it can be. For example, there's the story of Joseph and his coat of many colours...

Joseph wasn't like his brothers. They were down to earth, hard-working sheep farmers, keeping the business going. Joseph was a dreamer. A thinker. Not too good at the hard work – and yet their father loved Joseph so much that he gave him a wonderful coloured coat to wear. His brothers found this difficult to take. They wanted to kill him, even though one brother, Reuben, didn't want to go this far.

> ***Optional*** *Use some students to read the short extract or tell the story in your own words using the text below.*

Narrator Joseph's brothers were out in the remote countryside, looking after sheep, when Joseph came along.

Brother 1 Just look at him! The dreamer! All dressed up.

Brother 2 I've had enough of this. Let's kill him now. I can't stand him.

Brother 3 That'll put paid to his dreams. We can say he's been killed by animals.

Reuben No. We won't kill him. But we'll put him down this well.

Narrator The brothers put Joseph down the well. Reuben was planning to come back and rescue Joseph himself. But in the meantime, the brothers sold Joseph to a passing band of merchants who were on their way to Egypt.

Brother 1 Off he goes to Egypt. We'll never hear of him again.

Brother 2 No more dreams.

Brother 3 Father will have more time for us now.

Narrator Reuben was really upset when he realised Joseph had gone. The brothers killed a goat and dipped Joseph's coat in its blood. They then showed the coat to their father, to convince him that Joseph had been eaten by wild animals. But in Egypt, Joseph was moving towards a much higher destiny. He became the king's right-hand man and so powerful that many years later he was able to save his brothers' lives.

RESPONSE

Acknowledging failures and shortcomings

I want to suggest something to you. I want to suggest that each of us – you, me, the teachers, everyone – is jealous from time to time. Jealous of what someone has, what someone can do, what someone is. Remember we're not talking about admiring a person. Jealousy is when you say 'Why should she have that when I haven't. I'm going to take it out on her.'

It's difficult to acknowledge that you feel like that. But we have all felt like that at some time. Do you feel like that right now? *(Pause)* It's time for honesty. Let's be quiet and think about that for a while. *(Pause)*

Were you honest? If you were, and you understood your own feelings, then you are on your way to being more comfortable with yourself.

Commitment

Let me put something else to you. You don't need to be jealous. You are as valuable as anyone else. God knows that. We know that. That's what our school stands for. We don't want you to climb over other people to be popular. Be yourself. Be comfortable with yourself. You'll be happier for it, and you won't be making anyone else unhappy.

Extra Resources

The full story of Joseph and his brothers is in *Genesis*, chapter 37.

Music from *Joseph and the Technicolour Dreamcoat*.

Theme/ Key value

Bullying

Respect for others

Title

It's not your fault

Summary

Some bullied children believe that the problem lies with them – that bullying will stop if the victim changes the way he or she is. This assembly reinforces the view that it is the school's responsibility to protect its students from bullying, and that the school does not expect victims to shoulder the responsibility by changing their behaviour.

Resources

You need to have read Assemblies 1 and 2 of this theme.
Optional Students who have succeeded in any sphere – if at all possible they should be representative of the whole school community. Try to get a wide range and broad interpretation of achievement – helping in the community, sports, dance, drama, playing in a band for more than a month! School Behaviour Policy, if you have one. Three students if you chose the first.
Optional Any statements from school policy documents which assert the rights of others and respect for others.

REFLECTION

Remember the story about Rajinder? Well, here's the third part.

Why did Melanie and Naomi and Rachel bully Rajinder? Because she was different? Perhaps. After all, Rajinder does not like the same things that most people in the group like – she's not terribly interested in their kinds of music, nor is she too bothered about football teams.

So should Rajinder change?

Here are three possible pieces of advice we could give Rajinder. Listen to them, and try to decide which is right.

> ***Optional*** *Have each one of these printed separately to be handed to, and read out by, a different reader and/or to display on OHT. You could take the dramatisation further – have 'Rajinder' sitting in a chair, and each reader declaiming directly to her while she looks from one to the other trying to decide.*

Advice 1 Rajinder! Why be different? Try and be like everyone else! Get the right CDs. Get the right posters. Wear the right clothes in the evening and go to the right places. Then the other girls will think you are one of them and you can stop worrying about it. Don't be so aloof. Join in a bit more. Have a laugh! Get a life!

Advice 2 Rajinder! Be strong! Stand up to the bullies! Challenge them! Look them coolly in the eye before walking contemptuously away. If they threaten you, confront them. Never show you are upset. Never look frightened.

Advice 3 Rajinder! Why should you change? You're not the one doing something wrong! You have the right to be what you are, and if some people cannot accept that, then it's their problem, not yours. If they can't stop making your life difficult, then someone in the school must try and stop them.

Which advice is right?

> ***Optional*** *Advice 3 is the right one, but this should relate to school policy. Read any relevant policy statements.*

There are real dangers in asking someone to change because they are being bullied. It undermines what we stand for in this school, which is that everyone has the right to be the kind of person they want to be so long as they do not interfere with others.

■ *Refer to any school documents or statements that reinforce this.*

We stand for diversity. That means we enjoy our differences and we celebrate them. We'd like you to play your part in that – we'd like you to take pleasure in having different interests and different ideas. It's diversity and differences that make our school an interesting place to be.

Incidentally, we can apply the same principle to Melanie and her group, too. We want Melanie to stop bullying, but we don't want her to lose her confidence and sparkiness. And we certainly don't want her to change her interests. We want her to see that she can keep all that and stop this misery-making attitude towards Rajinder. When you think about it, it's just getting in the way of Melanie being the kind of pleasant and friendly girl that she really is. So it's important to realise that we accept Melanie – and Rachel, and Naomi. What we don't accept are bits of their behaviour that make someone else unhappy.

RESPONSE

Celebration of achievement

- *Use the assembly to celebrate different kinds of achievement in and out of school – to acknowledge people who have recently achieved something. Those who don't feel shy can come to the front for a handshake. Others may just be acknowledged where they sit. Teams might stand. You may wish just to do this verbally.*

  Or, if students are generally unwilling to be individually recognised, there can simply be a display recognising and celebrating achievement at the front of the hall.

There are many pathways to success. There is so much to admire here. Let's enjoy each success without jealousy or envy. Let's celebrate our diversity. *(Pause)*

Do we want people to change? *(Pause)* Do we want swimmers to change and be good dancers? We want to enjoy what everyone can do, without jealousy, without feeling inadequate, or feeling under pressure to do something that isn't in our nature.

Extra Resources

There is a wide range of publications associated with bullying.
Elliott, Michelle *Teenage Training Pack*. Available from Kidscape, World Trade Centre, Europe House, 3rd Floor, London E1 9AA.
For materials related to school and staff development, *Bullying: Schools do make a difference* published by Essex County Council Education Department (ISBN 0904 428 095) gives an excellent overview. There's also some useful poetry such as *Four O'Clock Friday* by John Foster, *Bully For You* by Ian Souter and *Bully Asleep* by John Walsh, all of which have been anthologised.

Theme/ Key value

Bullying

Respect for others

Title

Get you after school

Summary

The baggage which the phrase 'Get you after school' carries with it brings worry to students and parents and continual concern to heads and teachers. The threat itself can cause distress and disruption, even if there is no intent to carry it out. This assembly addresses some of these issues and invites students to reflect on effective ways of resolving conflict. It also raises the issue of the rights of others, which is treated as a separate theme in Secondary Assembly File.

Resources

Nothing at all.

REFLECTION

Let's look at some of the routes that you take home.

- *Go through some of the most generally used routes – the main walking and cycling routes, the location of the bus stops, school buses, trains as appropriate.*

Now it's honesty time. Have any of you ever gone a different way home to avoid meeting other students you were afraid of?

Would any of you put your hands up to that? You don't have to – but I know it happened to me when I was at school.

- *You could relate some appropriate personal experience here if you wish.*

I wonder if it's gone further than that? I wonder if anyone has been really late home because of going a long way round to avoid people?

Another question. I wonder if anyone here has ever been worried all day because someone has threatened to 'get' them after school? You know the expressions – 'Right – I'll get you on the way home.'

'Right – you're dead after school.'

A lot of the time, nothing happens. The threat is made, it worries you, and that's all. That's because the person making the threat knows there will be big trouble if he or she actually carries it out. That doesn't make the threatened person feel any better, though.

Now let me tell you something about rights and responsibilities. We in school believe that we all have some rights and we all have some responsibilities.

Let me remind you about some of your responsibilities.

- *Go through some of the school's expectations about attendance, punctuality, behaviour and respecting others.*

That's not the end of it, though. In return you have some rights.

One of them is the right to come to and from school by whichever route seems sensible and safe to you, without being threatened or stopped by anyone. That's your right. And it's our responsibility to see that you can do it. So if someone threatens you, so that you go home a different way, then they have taken away a basic right. Now I don't know about you, but I think that's serious.

Let me tell you about three people, in schools in Britain.

Let me tell you about Sean.

At nine o'clock one morning someone threatened to get him after school. At dinner time he went home without permission. There was nobody in, so he sat in the back garden and missed afternoon school. He missed football practice as well and was dropped from the cup game he had been looking forward to all term.

Let me tell you about Becky.

At ten o'clock one morning someone threatened to get her after school. She ran straight out at the end of school and went a very long way home. She arrived late to find that her mum was frantic, thinking that she was lost.

Let me tell you about Jock.

At morning break someone threatened to get him after school. He ran straight out after school and took a short cut across the railway. He was hit by a train and severely injured.

Some of the things that happen are serious, some are just annoying. But the point is they shouldn't happen at all.

RESPONSE

Commitment

Starting today, I want to try to remove altogether any fear of the journey home. That means we have to work together. You have to think about better ways of dealing with problems than 'get you after school'.

If you ever say to someone 'get you after school' it's an admission of failure. What you are saying is 'I can't think of a sensible way of settling this argument between us. So I'll do something stupid instead.'

But there are always unthinking people. The sensible ones have to deal with that.

How?

You have to keep an eye on each other. You have to remind each other of a basic right that's important to all of us. If your friend ever says, 'I'm afraid to go home,' then do something about it. Go home with them. Support them. That's what friendship is for. Then talk to us about it next day. Why should anyone have a basic right taken away?

I'm not going to forget that I've promised to support anyone in this school who is being bullied. That's my responsibility. I shall keep coming back to it, asking and talking. Don't you let me forget it either. Make a commitment to yourself – try and resolve your conflicts without threats.

Extra Resources

There is a wide range of publications associated with bullying.
Elliott, Michelle *Teenage Training Pack*. Available from Kidscape, World Trade Centre, Europe House, 3rd Floor, London E1 9AA.
For materials related to school and staff development, *Bullying: Schools do make a difference* published by Essex County Council Education Department (ISBN 0904 428 095) gives an excellent overview. There's also some useful poetry such as *Four O'Clock Friday* by John Foster, *Bully For You* by Ian Souter and *Bully Asleep* by John Walsh, all of which have been anthologised.

Theme/ Key value

Bullying

Respect for others

Title

Do they like doing it?

Summary

The evidence is that bullies do not 'delight' in making other people miserable. In fact, the inner feelings of bully and bullied are remarkably similar, and essentially have to do with lack of self-esteem – or self confidence if you prefer the term. This assembly uses this principle in an attempt to get bullies to reflect on how they might feel better if they tried other kinds of relationships.

Resources

Optional A confident reader in Year 8 or above to read the story.

REFLECTION

This is an assembly about how bullies feel. I'm going to begin with a short story based on fact.

> ***Optional*** *A confident reader could relate the story.*

Matt Williams was in Year 11 when Tara was in Year 8. Matt and his gang used to bully other kids. They would get money and food from them. Matt would just stand there, and two of his mates would get a kid in the corner and say, 'Here, what you got in your lunch box? Got a Mars bar have you?' And they'd get the Mars bar off the kid, and they always gave it to Matt, and he'd sort of sneer and say, 'Thanks kid!' in a really phoney accent that was supposed to sound really American and smart.

The funny thing was, Matt's gang never picked on girls. Tara couldn't understand why, but her sister could. She was in Year 11, the same as Matt. She laughed when Tara asked if she was afraid of him. 'Afraid of Matt? You're joking. He's just sad, is Matt.'

Tara thought a lot about what her sister said after that. She said Matt was 'sad'. Tara knew she meant sad in a particular way – she meant pathetic, ineffective. But Tara started to think of other meanings of the word 'sad'... She thought how sad can mean unhappy.

You see, Matt wasn't really happy. You never saw him having a laugh – oh, he called it 'having a laugh' when he bullied other kids, but his face wasn't bright and happy in the way that Tara's sister's was, for example.

It all came to a head when Tara found herself sitting next to Matt on a coach. Matt's English group were being taken off to see a play, and there were some spare seats, so the head said some of the teacher's students from lower down the school could go. The teacher, Mr Grayson, was really strict. He was so confident and in control.

Anyway, he made everyone sit on the coach where he said, and he sat Matt right at the front in the seat behind him, and he sat Tara with Matt. None of his gang were in that English group anyway – Tara thought the school organised it like that.

Matt scowled at Tara a couple of times. Then Tara just plunged in and started chatting to him quite normally. 'Where are you going for your holidays, Matt?' she asked. He looked quite surprised. 'Majorca,' he said. After a bit he really got talking about Majorca. His mum took him every year. He went on and on about Majorca. 'It's brilliant!' he said. 'We have this apartment, and the beach is across the road, and you can swim all the time, or sunbathe – and the night life's pretty good, too!' It was quite interesting really.

So they all went to the play – it was really boring – and back again, and Tara chatted to Matt all the time. And do you know he was really nice. He said, 'See you around' when they parted.

Matt was still a bully afterwards but Tara wasn't frightened any more. She felt quite sorry for Matt really – and for all his hangers-on. They were no more happy than the kids they bullied.

So why did they do it? Why couldn't they make proper friends?

That's the question isn't it? Why did they do it? You know bullies aren't happy with what they are doing.

Come on, honesty time. Are you a bully? Ever? Does it make you happy? Does it make you feel good inside? Of course it doesn't. You might get a little surge of excitement and pleasure, but there's nothing there when that's gone.

What makes people feel good is having real friends who can be generous to you, and make you warm inside. Being a bully doesn't get you friends like that.

RESPONSE

Commitment

I want you to think about these two ideas.

First, that we all want to feel better about ourselves.

Let's be silent for a moment and think about that. Think about ways in which you would like to improve. *(Pause)*

Second, that the funny thing is that sometimes we try to make ourselves feel better by making other people feel worse.

Let's be silent again and think about that. Making somebody else feel worse may give you a burst of excitement, but it really won't make you feel any better about yourself. How can it? *(Pause)*

Some of the best moments come from seeing a big smile come to the face of someone else – how do you feel when you tickle your baby cousin and she laughs and giggles?

How do you feel when your mum opens the present you gave her?

How do you feel when your best friend smiles to see you come into the room? Is your world like that?

Or is your world made up of putting other people down and upsetting them? Today, try to change your world into one that you can enjoy.

Extra Resources

There is a wide range of publications associated with bullying.

Elliott, Michelle *Teenage Training Pack*. Available from Kidscape, World Trade Centre, Europe House, 3rd Floor, London E1 9AA.

Foster, J (1992) *Issues 1*. Collins Educational Unit 7, Bullying pp32–7.

Tattum, D & Herbert, G (1990) *Bullying: A positive response.* Cardiff, South Glamorgan Institue of Higher Education.

For materials related to school and staff development, *Bullying: Schools do make a difference* published by Essex County Council Education Department (ISBN 0904 428 095) gives an excellent overview. There's also some useful poetry such as *Four O'Clock Friday* by John Foster, *Bully For You* by Ian Souter and *Bully Asleep* by John Walsh, all of which have been anthologised.

Theme

Barriers

Assemblies on this theme

1 Barriers of age
This assembly uses a real-life holiday incident to challenge some commonly-held prejudices about old age.

2 Barriers of war
This assembly uses the account of an extraordinary incident during the Second World War to show that whatever the politics of war, the people who fight for their country are ordinary people.

3 Images of gender
This assembly encourages young people to be aware of gender-stereotyping and to challenge it where necessary.

4 Religious clothing
This assembly uses the example of religiously symbolic clothing to illustrate religious discrimination.

5 The new taboo – HIV and AIDS
The tale of St Francis and the leprosy sufferer is used to challenge attitudes towards people with HIV and AIDS.

Record of use

Taken by	1	2	3	4	5
Date					
Given to					

Comments

pfp, 61 Gray's Inn Road, London WC1X 8TL May be photocopied for use within the purchasing institution only.

pfp, 61 Gray's Inn Road, London WC1X 8TL May be photocopied for use within the purchasing institution only.

Theme/ Key value

Barriers

Valuing truth/having an open mind

Title

Barriers of age

Summary

This assembly uses a real-life holiday incident to challenge some commonly-held prejudices about old age.

Resources

Nothing at all.

REFLECTION

A middle-aged British couple sat at a pavement cafe outside a smart restaurant in the south of France. As they sipped their drinks and watched the world go by, a motorcycle drew up on the opposite side of the street. The husband looked across in envy at the machine. It was a Honda Goldwing, a huge tourer with roomy panniers behind the passenger seat. He'd had a motorbike himself when he was young – nothing that grand, but not bad. But once they had got married and had the kids, they needed a car and the bike had had to go.

The wife, meanwhile, looked across the street in envy at the two riders dismounting from the Goldwing. A man and a woman, their slim figures neat as models in their gold and black leathers. She'd been quite slim herself once. But she never seemed to get her figure back after having the children, and then there'd been the final lost battle against middle-aged spread.

As the British couple watched them, each with their own private envy, the leather-clad bikers took off their helmets and walked across to the tables of the pavement cafe. And never have two holiday-makers had such a mind-boggling surprise. For the bikers who now sat down at the table next to them were not young at all. They were very obviously well past seventy, both with short cropped white hair, tanned faces and relaxed smiles.

In pretty good English, they explained that they lived north of Paris, and they used a car through the winter. But every year they spent their summer months on the motorbike, visiting places they'd always longed to see but never managed to get to while they were working.

That's a true story and it shows how wrong you can be when you have set ideas about any group of people – in this case, the elderly.

When you're a teenager, people in their twenties are rated okay, and even some people in their thirties. But after that there's a kind of barrier beyond which people are definitely old. I bet a few of you think your parents are old, out of touch and past it!

But I also bet most of your parents don't think they're old! People their age think they won't be old until they reach retirement age. And if you talk to people who are aged between sixty and seventy-five – well most of them don't think they're old either! Most retired people only start thinking of themselves as 'elderly' after they've turned eighty.

Postponing 'being old' like this is actually a very Western way of looking at age. The Hindu scriptures teach that life is divided up into four stages, each lasting twenty-five years, and you just move from one stage to the next.

- In stage one, you concentrate on education and establishing yourself in your job.
- In stage two, you bring up your family.
- In stage three – when you're fifty – you start getting used to the idea that your

life on Earth won't last for ever. Strictly speaking, the Hindu scriptures recommend that you should give up your job, give away your wealth and move into a smaller, more modest home.

- Stage four is for really devout Hindu men. At seventy-five, they leave home to become 'holy men' and concentrate on a life of prayer and meditation, living by begging. Other holy men may even hold a mock funeral to show that that person has already left this life.

Here in the West, we don't see life in stages like that. We want to be young for ever! But this emphasis on staying young can breed some harmful attitudes. It's easy to think that it's only possible to live life to the full if you're young and that entering old age is giving in to a disease which robs you of your health, your strength, your intelligence, your sense of humour and your ambition.

Okay, there are some old people who are ill or unhappy or bitter about being old. But there are also many who aren't. Old age actually has a lot going for it. Once you retire from work, you've got time to do all the things you couldn't do before when work had to come first. And giving up work doesn't mean giving up all your interests and hobbies – you've actually got more time to pursue them. If someone has been fairly active all their life, they're likely to remain active in their retirement.

The other thing to remember is that with high unemployment rates, people can sometimes choose to retire as early as fifty – or are made redundant and can't get a job again. Just because you're retired doesn't mean you're old.

It's sad that we tend to think that life is over for people who have retired. We look at them as people who aren't worth as much as others. It's easy to forget that they are a vital part of the whole community, with special gifts which only come with age. People who've lived a long time can have a wisdom about the way the world works which could benefit younger people. Many of them have the kind of maturity you only get from having survived all the knocks life can throw at you.

In previous generations in this country, old people were respected for their superior experience much more than they seem to be now. It's often the Asian families in Britain, some of whom are Hindu, who remind us that our old people are an asset. Asian family 'elders' are almost always treated with deep respect by their families, who value the maturity, wisdom and overview of the world they have from the experience of their years.

RESPONSE

Celebration and thankfulness

We have a lot to be proud of in this school when it comes to challenging old prejudices such as racial prejudice and religious prejudice.

Acknowledging failure and shortcomings

But maybe old age is an area where we do still think of some people as a 'group', all the same, not as individuals. *(Pause.)* Age can create barriers which make communication difficult between the generations and which can lead to discrimination and misunderstanding.

Commitment

I hope after today's assembly you'll make some commitment to look at age differences in a different light – with more of an open mind. Think a bit harder about the 'old' people you know. When you get a chance, ask them about their lives. I bet they'll surprise you.

Extra Resources

Sanders, P (1991) *What it's like to be old*, Aladdin Books.

Theme/ Key value

Barriers

Valuing truth/having an open mind

Title

Barriers of war

Summary

This assembly uses the account of an extraordinary incident during the Second World War to show that whatever the politics of war, the people who fight for their country are ordinary people. Warning: you may wish to avoid the term 'bastards' in the extract on the next page.

Resources

Supplied OHT image (p36).
Optional A student to read the Russian boy's account. Please note that it is a very moving passage and it is important that it's read by a good and sensitive reader.

REFLECTION

■ *Show supplied OHT image.*

Soon after you started school, I imagine a good number of you found yourself as part of a set of friends – a 'gang', some people might have called it. You probably had a rival gang too – your enemies.

This might still go on a bit now. Older children – and adults too – sometimes form themselves into rival gangs who see each other as 'the enemy' and even engage in various kinds of warfare. This often just involves a lot of posing and posturing, but sometimes it can involve real injury or even death. Remember the terrible death of the London headteacher killed at Christmas 1995 as he was trying to save one of his students who was being attacked by a gang.

But how many of you have later become friends with someone who was once your sworn enemy? It happens quite often. And it happens because people's hatred is often focussed on groups, but when they meet an individual from that group they realise they're just an ordinary person. The sort of person you could actually like.

That's something which has happened for a long, long time. Some of you may be studying 'Romeo and Juliet'. You'll know that this typifies what Shakespeare was talking about all those years ago. It didn't matter that Romeo and Juliet were from rival families. When they met, they liked each other. In fact they fell in love.

When countries go to war, the gangs get much bigger. Whole nations become suspicious of other whole nations. The 'them and us' thing takes on disasterous dimensions. Suddenly, the propaganda tells only the bad things of 'them' and people stop thinking about what individuals are really like. They forget that most of them are just people going to school, going to work, going shopping, eating, drinking and playing just the same as most other people in the world.

Someone once wrote that the first casualty of war is truth. *(Pause.)* Recently, in the war in Bosnia, communities with different ethnic origins, who had lived as neighbours and friends for generations, were suddenly thrown into conflict and hatred. The scars of that terrible conflict haven't healed yet. *(Pause.)*

In 1939, at the beginning of the Second World War, Germany and Britain were enemies. At the same time, Germany and what was then the Soviet Union were friends. However, over the next couple of years, their peace pact looked increasingly less permanent until, in June 1941, Germany suddenly invaded Russia.

The two largest armies in the world were now locked in combat on a battle front which stretched for two thousand miles, with tragic results. Many hundreds of thousands of men were killed on both sides. Civilians died of starvation. Eventually, the fierce Russian winter worked in the Russians' favour. The defeated German attackers were rounded up and marched through the streets of Moscow.

This is a quote from a Russian boy who watched the parade.

"In 1941 Mama took me back to Moscow. There I saw our enemies for the first time. If my memory is right, nearly twenty thousand German war prisoners were to be marched in a single column through the streets of Moscow.

The pavements swarmed with onlookers, cordoned off by soldiers and police.

The crowd were mostly women – Russian women with hands roughened by hard work, lips untouched by lipstick and thin hunched shoulders which had borne half the burden of the war. Every one of them must have had a father or a husband, a brother or a son killed by the Germans.

They gazed with hatred in the direction from which the column was to appear.

At last we saw it.

The generals marched at the head, massive chins stuck out, lips folded disdainfully, their whole demeanour meant to show superiority over their plebian victors.

"They smell of eau-de-cologne, the bastards," someone in the crowd said with hatred.

The women were clenching their fists. The soldiers and policemen had all they could do to hold them back.

All at once, something happened to them.

They saw German soldiers, thin, unshaven, wearing dirty bloodstained bandages, hobbling on crutches or leaning on the shoulders of their comrades; the soldiers walked with their heads down.

The street became dead silent – the only sound was the shuffling of boots and the thumping of crutches.

Then I saw an elderly woman in broken-down boots push herself forward and touch a policeman's shoulder, saying: 'Let me through.' There must have been something about her that made him step aside.

She went up to the column, took from inside her coat something wrapped in a coloured handkerchief and unfolded it. It was a crust of black bread. She pushed it awkwardly into the pocket of a German soldier, so exhausted that he was tottering on his feet. And now suddenly from every side women were running towards the soldiers, pushing into their hands bread, cigarettes, whatever they had.

The soldiers were no longer enemies.

They were people."

RESPONSE

Gangs, tribes, groups, communities, nations – we all seem to need to belong to some grouping. But let's not confuse that with thinking 'they' are to be hated or feared. We're all people with our strengths and frailties and we should try to remember that.

Commitment

Here is an old Jewish prayer. Whether or not you have a faith yourself, you can recognise within these words the deep desire to find a way for people to live together in peace, and perhaps identify with that desire yourself.

'May it be thy will, O Lord, that no man foster hatred against us in his heart, and that we foster no hatred in our hearts against any man; that no man foster envy of us in his heart, and that we foster no envy in our hearts of any man.' *(From the Talmud.)*

Extra Resources

The extract is from *A Precocious Autobiography* by Yevgeny Yevtushenko published by HarperCollins.

Flint, D (1994) *Hot off the press: Bosnia*, Aladdin Books.

Theme/ Key value

Barriers

Valuing truth/having an open mind

Title

Images of gender

Summary

This assembly encourages young people to be aware of gender-stereotyping and to challenge it where necessary.

Resources

Supplied OHT image (p36).

REFLECTION

Here in school we're concerned about what we think and believe. We're in a community that's *(name of your school).* Two of the values of our community are that we try to respect others and that we're totally against any kind of prejudice. It doesn't matter what colour or sex people are, we aim to treat everyone equally.

I hope that most of you understand and agree with those values too, and try to keep to them. But it's not always easy is it? I'm sure at some time or another many of you have found yourselves thinking, saying or doing things that aren't in line with those values, even though you do agree with them. Let's take the example of what gender people are. Let's try to think of some reasons why it might be that we find ourselves making assumptions about men and women based on their gender, when we know that they are as capable – or not! – as each other.

Think about the images you have around you every day. What about computer games? They're commonplace these days. I expect there's a good number of you who have games of some kind at home.

When something is so widespread, it's quite valid to ask questions about it – about why it's good and why it's bad – because it's likely to have an influence on us. One of the questions we can ask about video games is about the kind of messages which their images give us. One of the things found in a recent survey was that most of the images of women in computer games show them as victims and very rarely as heroes.

There's no conclusive evidence that playing computer games or watching particular films actually makes people do certain things, although many people are working hard to try and find out if it does – it's a very difficult thing to measure. But even if they don't actually affect what we do – do they affect what we think? What these images are doing is confirming the idea that men and women have particular roles in life just because of their gender.

The super hi-tech computer games seem in fact to be turning the clock back to an age when girls were expected to play with dolls while boys played with guns, when dad had to work while mum stayed at home, when it was natural for women to cry when they were sad, but for men to keep a stiff upper lip. A society which says 'only men can do that' or 'only women can do this' is a society inhibited by barriers which stop people from being themselves and discovering their full potential.

Pigeonholing men and women into set roles is called 'gender-stereotyping'. Over the years, people of both sexes have fought hard and long to break down gender-stereotyping barriers.

For example, before 1870 girls weren't allowed to take the exams to get into university – the equivalent of today's A Levels. The respected medical journal *The Lancet* even said 'Giving them a boy's education will damage their reproductive organs'! But girls fought back and, obviously, have proved them wrong.

Women in this country couldn't vote before 1918, and even then it was only the privilege of a few. The vote wasn't given to all women until 1928.

Men had their battles too. In a world where men were supposed to be the tough bread-winners and women were the gentle carers, it was a brave man who had the courage to turn the tables and go into nursing, for example.

Two World Wars did much to change people's attitudes about who could do what. In times of war, women kept the railways running and worked in factories and on farms. Men nursed the wounded and comforted the dying.

But although it did begin to show people what they could and couldn't do, it didn't put a stop to gender-stereotyping. As late as the 1980s, most mixed schools had a curriculum in which only girls learned to cook and only boys used tools at the workbench. Your parents may well remember this – perhaps you could ask them what it was like at their school.

In 1975, Parliament set up the Equal Opportunities Commission to promote equality of opportunity between men and women. But the law doesn't change attitudes. Society as a whole is still coming to terms with gender equality.

When you go to a department store, the baby-feeding and changing rooms are usually somewhere within the ladies toilet! What if a man's looking after the baby?

We all fall into the gender-stereotyping trap from time to time. There's a very good children's book which exploits this human weakness to great effect. Some of you may know it – *The Turbulent Term of Tyke Tyler* by Gene Kemp. If so, I wonder if you were caught out at the end? It is written so cleverly that is makes us fall into making assumptions, and then catches us out.

■ *Show supplied OHT image.*

And that's the heart of the problem. We all make automatic assumptions without thinking about the barriers those assumptions are building for people. If we automatically assume that a nurse is always a woman and a soldier is always a man, we're denying thousands of people a basic human right – the right to discover their own full potential as a person, regardless of gender.

Optional with KS4 students

I'm going to leave you with a couple of questions to think about. First, why do *some* men feel the need to see women as victims, as less capable than men or as more vulnerable? And second, why do *some* women seem to accept that role of vulnerable partner and victim?

RESPONSE

Commitment and action

At the beginning of the assembly, we talked about our school values. We recognise that there are physical and psychological differences between males and females, but that doesn't mean that they're not equal. There's a phrase which sums this up – 'different therefore equal'. Just because someone is different, it doesn't mean that they are better or worse. It is no reason for prejudice. Remember, it's usually weak people who need to look for a group they can believe is inferior.

In this school you're not barred from your favourite lesson or discouraged from applying for a good job, because of your sex. Also we believe in treating males and females equally. Just think about that – now and the next time you hear others making assumptions about men and women. In your own life, make sure you treat all people fairly, and that you don't help those prejudices to survive. *(Pause.)*

Extra Resources

The survey referred to was by Eugene Provenzo and was reported in the *Media Awareness Project Bulletin* (November, 1995).

Theme/ Key value

Barriers

Valuing truth/having an open mind

Title

Religious clothing

Summary

This assembly uses the example of religiously symbolic clothing to illustrate religious discrimination. Please note that it is based on the assumption that the school has a uniform. If your school doesn't, it will need to be adapted slightly (para 4 in particular).

Resources

Nothing at all.

REFLECTION

If you've got friends who go to other schools, perhaps you sometimes talk about how things are done there as compared with here. Not just how the lessons are taught or what facilities there are, but what the school 'ethos' is like. *(Include features from your school in the following.)* For example, are rules imposed from above or are they fixed by a council of students and teachers together? What systems are used to make sure there's the right kind of discipline? If there are school prefects, are they seen as helpful or elitist? And the age old question – what difference does it make having a school uniform?

Let's think a bit more about that last one. You wear uniforms almost all the time really, although you might not always see it like that. If you're playing sport, you wear tracksuits or shorts and T-shirts and trainers – or a team strip. If you're going for a night out, you dress up in something fashionable. If you're going round to a friend's house to listen to music or watch videos, you probably all wear jeans or whatever comfy clothing you like to lounge around in. You wear particular clothes which suit particular activities – they're all uniforms really.

And you do that not just so that you're comfortable or you look right, but because it makes you feel right too – it makes you feel like doing the activity you're dressing up for.

That's one of the main reasons why you're required to wear school uniform and why you're stopped from wearing other things. We want everyone to be comfortable, but we also want our school to feel like a place where we're working and learning. So we come to school in our working and learning clothes. By wearing these clothes, we know that that's what we're here to do – we know that we're not here to relax in front of the TV, or to shop, or to go for a night out.

But there are a few times when school uniform is adapted slightly – when we allow people to combine their working and learning uniform with another one.

Many students all over the country don't just go to school, they are also part of religious communities. At one time, most children in British schools were followers of the Christian faith, but for many years now, Britain has been a multi-cultural, multi-faith society. In our school here today, we have some (*many*) students who follow another *(other*) religious faith(*s*). And, of course, we have students who have chosen not to follow any particular religion.

As you would expect, it's not necessarily obvious which people are members of a particular religion and which aren't. Belief is very much a matter of personal commitment of the mind and heart. But many religions do have uniforms of a kind – particular dress codes which are sometimes compulsory and sometimes not, but which people follow out of respect for and devotion to their faith.

Christians remember that their founder, Jesus Christ, was executed by being nailed to a wooden cross, and many of them choose to wear a tiny cross – usually of gold or silver – on a neck-chain. Would it be right to stop them?

Jewish men wear a shawl and a skull cap to say their prayers. Some Jewish men wear their cap – the 'yarmulka' – all the time as a sign of respect before God. So naturally, there are Jewish young men and boys who would want to wear their yarmulka at school. Would it be right to stop them?

The Muslim holy book, the *Qu'ran*, teaches that women should dress modestly, covering not just their bodies, but also their heads and their legs. This way of dressing is called 'hijab'. Muslim girls living in Britain often observe hijab by wearing a headscarf (shalwar), trousers (kameez) and a tunic at school. Would it be right to stop them?

Committed members of the Sikh religion are initiated into a 'brotherhood', which these days can include girls as well as boys. There are special clothes and objects which have to be worn every day as reminders of their commitment to the brotherhood. A metal bangle or a pair of shorts under ordinary clothes wouldn't cause comment. But there's also a small dagger. And the boys don't ever cut their hair – they twist it, fix it with a special comb and cover it with a turban. Would it be right to stop them?

The things people wear to symbolise their faith are a little different from other uniforms. Faith isn't something which you do for an hour or so and then finish. For people who have a faith, it's something which is with them all the time. We respect that commitment, which is why we respect their wish to wear things which symbolise it, and why we don't allow those symbols to act as barriers which stop us being aware of the person behind them.

Sensitivity and courtesy are a part of our school ethos. We might question the motives of someone who comes to school in something straight out of a fashion show. But do we have the right to create barriers or question the motives of anyone – whether here in school or anywhere else – who is wearing a symbol of devotion to their chosen religion?

RESPONSE

Acknowledging failure and shortcomings

It's the easiest thing in the world to put barriers up because of what people look like and what they wear, and to make fun of them. It doesn't take any thought or effort. It usually just means that the person making fun is too lazy or shallow, or frightened perhaps, to take the time to go behind the surface to find out if that person is a good person or not – good fun, good friend, good anything.

If you feel like that then you're losing out on something important – having an open mind.

Celebration and thankfulness

There's something to be thankful for here.

There are the new insights we get from being with people whose beliefs are different from our own. These beliefs bring a refreshing variety to our school and our society. If you are a member of a particular religion, you can take pride in its signs and symbols.

(Pause.) All of us, whether or not we are religious, can take pride in always showing respect for other people's beliefs and having an open mind.

Extra Resources

The World Religions series (1995) ,Wayland.

Mayled, J (1987) *Religious Topics: Religious Symbols*, Wayland.

Theme/ Key value

Barriers

Valuing truth/having an open mind

Title

The new taboo – HIV and AIDS

Summary The tale of St Francis and the leprosy sufferer is used to challenge attitudes towards people with HIV and AIDS.

Resources Supplied OHT image (p36).

REFLECTION

Francesco Bernadone was a rich young nobleman who lived in Italy at the end of the 12th century. His father was a wealthy cloth merchant and the young Francesco – or Francis – lived the life of a prince. He had fine clothes and fine horses, and was used to entertaining and being entertained with the best food and wine money could buy. Among the rich social set of Assisi, the town where he lived, Francis was the undisputed leader.

But Assisi had its poor side too. Hidden away between the elegant houses of the nobles and the merchants were filthy little rooms, squalor, disease and misery. In those days, there was little hope for the sick or disabled. For most of them, the only chance of help was to beg outside the churches and houses of the rich, in the hope of a coin being flung at them.

Young Francis certainly saw the twisted limbs, the sores and dirty rags, and in spite of the perfume which scented his own fine clothes and the smell of the wine he had drunk, the stench of poverty and illness sickened him. He especially shrank away from people with the dreaded skin disease, leprosy.

But seeing poverty like that troubled the young nobleman, and, before long, he began to find ways of helping the poor. He gave them money, he paid for their medicines, he even brought them home for huge meals when his father was away on business! But he still felt he wasn't doing enough. He began to feel that he was being called to give his whole life to living with the poor – as one of them.

He prayed that God would show him what he had to do with his life. Soon afterwards, he was was riding near Assisi when suddenly to his horror he saw a man with leprosy in his path and the old loathing rose up and choked him. Normally, he would have yielded to his fear and swerved aside on his horse, flinging a coin to the poor wretch. But this time, he found a power within him which was stronger than his fear. He jumped off his horse, approached the man and put the money into his hand. Then he gently took the hand and kissed it, putting his lips to the rotting flesh.

That encounter was the turning point for Francis. He gave his life to living in poverty and serving others. Before long, his gentleness and sincerity attracted a brotherhood of followers around him who all shared his concern for the poor and the sick.

For thousands of years, leprosy was a terrifying disease. It rotted away the flesh of the sufferer. Because no-one really understood how it was caught, and no-one had a cure, people with leprosy were avoided like the plague. So they suffered not only from the pain of their illness, but also from being shunned and isolated by people filled with fear. A fear that often came out as hate and blame, so that leprosy sufferers were excluded from normal society. They begged at city gates and worshipped by squinting through special slits cut into church walls.

Modern medicine has made life immeasurably better for leprosy sufferers.

The disease can be quickly diagnosed and halted and, in severe cases, plastic surgery can restore withered limbs.

But we've got another group of people today who feel the double pain of an incurable disease and isolation from a fearful society. This fear, as before, often expresses itself as hate and blame. At the end of the twentieth century, if you're known to be HIV-positive, you can still be made to feel as if you must live outside the city like a medieval leper, begging at the gates and squinting through church walls from the cold outside.

Even if you don't have AIDS, try going for a job if you're HIV-positive and don't like telling lies. Nobody wants you. And because you're not registered disabled, the company is under no obligation to employ you. Parents with AIDS live with another permanent terror. They dread seeing their children spat at in the playground, or having other parents boycotting the school until their own child is withdrawn.

Thankfully, there are still people around like St Francis – people who are prepared to overcome prejudice and the barriers set up against AIDS sufferers and their families. But their work is often the target of discrimination. When one school 'adopted' a local family affected by AIDS (a family not known to them), they ran a sponsored stay-awake to raise money for them. But many people asked if the AIDS in this family had come through haemophilia, and when they were told it hadn't, they refused to sponsor the effort. There's a common assumption that HIV and AIDS are disorders confined to homosexuals and drug addicts. In fact, the latest figures show that new cases have slowed down in these groups. The real increase is now among non-drug-using heterosexuals.

Ignorance of the facts fans the flames of fear and hatred. People with AIDS are sometimes driven from where they live after repeated attacks on them and their homes.

The sad thing is that the fear behind such hatred is now known to be completely unfounded. There's virtually no chance of catching the AIDS virus except through unprotected sex with a carrier or through using a syringe which has been used by a carrier.

People with HIV and AIDS don't need the kind of medieval hatred and blame which once isolated leprosy sufferers of old. They need the best medical care available, and the kind of genuine fellow-feeling which once brought a proud nobleman down off his high horse to kiss a diseased hand.

RESPONSE

Commitment and action

■ *Show supplied OHT image.*

When someone you love is dying, you suffer too as you watch them and care for them. Think for a moment of people today who are doing just that – parents, partners, children or friends. If you have a faith, you may like to say a short prayer for them. *(Pause.)*

With AIDS, it's not just the disease which causes pain. The hurt of discrimination causes deep wounds. Perhaps the most cruel wounds are those inflicted on young children because of their parent's illness. *(Pause.)* Our responsibility in this school is

- to be informed
- not to add to all the misinformation
- to have the courage to challenge those who want to build the barriers which only serve needlessly to add to the pain.

Extra Resources

Information is available from The Terrence Higgins Trust, 52–54 Grays Inn Road, London WC1X 8BR. School packs for helping local families are available from ACET (AIDS Care Education and Training) – regional addresses available from local telephone directories.

Theme

Conservation

Assemblies on this theme

1 Life depends on water
This assembly illustrates some examples of water pollution and encourages students to consider ways of reducing the problem. It needs some preparation.

2 Like a dog in a car – global warming
This assembly uses the example of a dog in a car to explore the idea of personal responsibility in the matter of global warming.

3 Whose is all this junk?
This assembly uses a short humorous sketch to illustrate the point that waste management is a personal problem.

4 Junk in space
This assembly introduces the issue of extra-terrestrial pollution in the form of space junk.

5 One man's meat...
This assembly uses interviews with students who are vegetarian to highlight some of the environmental issues which vegetarianism addresses.

Record of use

Taken by	1	2	3	4	5
Date					
Given to					

Comments

 ISBN 1 874050 39 2

Theme/ Key value

Conservation

Respect for the living environment

Title

Life depends on water

Summary

This assembly illustrates some examples of water pollution and encourages students to consider ways of reducing the problem. It needs some preparation.

Resources

Supplied OHT image (p48). A large pot plant. A large clear-glass jug half-filled with water and a tumbler. ***Optional*** A large grocery box containing: a bottle of liquid fertilizer, a bottle of liquid detergent, a bag of loose soil, a can of lubricating oil and a child's plastic potty containing some cold weak tea or coffee. **Note** – if you do not use the optional resources, the assembly will need adapting slightly.

REFLECTION

Today's assembly is about respecting the living environment. That means everything which is alive on our planet, but it doesn't just mean the things people usually think of when they talk about this issue, such as rainforests, deserts, animals threatened with extinction and so on. No, it means things much closer to home, and school, and much closer to you. I want you to leave assembly today thinking about one of those things – water.

Who had a cup of tea or coffee this morning? Who had a fruit juice? Who had a can of something? (*Pause.*) Who had a glass of water? Thank you.

Nutritionists – the people who know which foods are good for us – say we don't drink enough water. Apparently, in some countries, people drink more canned drinks than plain water. In fact, there could well be some of us here who drink more canned drinks than plain water! However, despite what you might have heard, the tap water in this country is pure enough to drink. And, in case you need convincing of that, I'll just have a little drink of tap water from this jug.

■ *Pour some water from the jug into the glass, take a sip and then empty the glass on to the pot plant.*

I thought the plant looked thirsty, too! Now just to prove that this tap water is perfectly harmless, I'd like someone else to come up and take a little sip too.

■ *Pour a tiny drink from the jug into the tumbler and ask the volunteer to drink it.* ***Optional*** *Ask him/her to stay with you to help.*

Nearly three-quarters of the Earth's surface is covered with water. All life on our planet depends on it. Fortunately, water is usually easy to come by for most people. You get it from rain, springs, wells, streams, rivers, ponds and lakes. And of course it also fills the vast ocean beds.

Water. All life depends on it. Did you know that

- 60% of your body weight is water.
- A watermelon is 92% water.
- An egg is 74% water.
- A piece of lean meat is 70% water.
- When you take a bath, you sit in up to a hundred litres of water.
- A shower uses twenty litres a minute.
- It takes nine litres of water to refine one litre of petrol?

We couldn't live without it.

The sad thing is, we're not very good at looking after the Earth's water supply. Since the beginning of civilisation, water has been used to carry away unwanted rubbish. For endless centuries, humans have been dumping waste in rivers, streams, lakes and oceans. Until recently, this wasn't a problem, because many materials, especially organic materials, decompose in water. They are what we

 ISBN 1 874050 39 2

now call 'bio-degradable'. Water becomes polluted when there is an accumulation of non-bio-degradable materials. Things like metals, plastics and chemicals.

The pollution doesn't just happen when the offending substance is put into the water. Some chemicals begin a deadly chain reaction. For example, we use fertilizers to make plants grow. *(**Optional** Pour some liquid fertilizer into the jug.)*

These plant nutrients find their way through the soil into streams, rivers and lakes, making algae grow like crazy. When the algae die, they cause an oxygen deficiency, which means the aquatic animal life dies as well. With no creatures in the water to eat the plant life it spreads rapidly, which soon reduces the amount of open water. It's only a matter of time before a whole lake becomes dry land.

And it's not just the farmers using large amounts of fertilizers – it's us too, because these same chemicals are also used in some household detergents. *(**Optional** Pour liquid detergent into the jug.)*

Clean water isn't so easy to come by after all. Almost every country in the world is working on ways of using water efficiently. In this country in 1995 we had droughts – even though so much rain falls on Britain. Using less water not only saves money, it helps save the environment. Every time you flush the toilet, leave a tap running or fill up the bath, you're doing something which may be a luxury in the future. In the last hundred and fifty years of industrial development, factories have turned waterways into open sewers by dumping oils, toxic chemicals and other harmful industrial waste into them, with devastating effects on the fish life. In our city streets, rain mixes with the oil and grime and runs off into drains which empty into canals and rivers. (***Optional** Pour some lubricating oil into the jug.*)

And – incredibly – some seaside towns still empty human sewage straight into the sea where children swim. *(**Optional** Pour the contents of the child's potty into the jug. Be ready for the reaction from the spectators!)*

Now I wonder if my helper is still thirsty? (***Optional** Pour some 'polluted' water into the tumbler and offer it. When it's refused, make as if to pour it on the pot-plant. You will almost certainly be stopped.)*

No – I couldn't do it, even to a plant. And we shouldn't do it to the Earth, either. *(**Optional** Dismiss the helper.)*

In many religions water symbolises cleansing and purity. Hindu and Buddhist children have special baths to wash in. The waters of the River Ganges in India are holy to millions of Indians. Muslims wash as part of their preparations for prayer. All around the world, water is a symbol of cleanliness – yet we continue to dirty it, making it into the world's waste bucket.

RESPONSE

Acknowledging failure and shortcomings

■ *Show supplied OHT image.*

If we're honest, we've all added to the problem of water pollution to some extent. We're the ones who eat the crops sprayed with chemical nutrients. *(Pause.)* We're the ones who wear the clothes washed with chemical detergents. *(Pause.)*

Action

Perhaps there may be openings at home for suggesting different shopping priorities. *(Pause.)* If our planet is to support life for generations after ours, we have to do things to make it happen. *(Pause.)*

Extra Resources

New Internationalist, No 273 (November, 1995)
Leggett, D (1991) *Troubled Waters*, Templar.
Bennett, P (1993) *Earth: The Incredible Recycling Machine*, Wayland.

Theme/ Key value

Conservation

Respect for the living environment

Title

Like a dog in a car – global warming

Summary

This assembly uses the example of a dog in a car to explore the idea of personal responsibility in the matter of global warming.

Resources

Supplied OHT image (p48).

REFLECTION

It was a warm summer morning when Dawn Springworth drove into town to her favourite hairdresser. It was a bit of an occasion, because she was having her hair cut, coloured and permed ready for her wedding the following week. She parked in the shade in the long-stay car park next to the council offices – the council employees didn't use it on Saturdays. As a deterrent against car-thieves, she left her dog in the car. But Dawn was so preoccupied with all her pre-wedding arrangements, she did what she had never done before. She locked the car and walked away without leaving a window open.

It was three hours before she returned to find her precious little terrier in a collapsed state from which he never recovered. Once the sun had begun to shine on to the car, the heat inside had built up unmercifully until the dog was overcome by heat-stroke and dehydration. *(Pause)*

Perhaps you've come across similar stories in the news. There have even been occasions when small children have died in cars left in the sun. The glass windows let in sunlight which then heats up everything inside the car. But the window glass doesn't let heat out again. More sunlight, more heat, no ventilation, higher and higher temperatures, drastic results.

The more often we hear about it, the more likely we are to be careful ourselves and never leave an animal or child in a car in the sun.

But in one way, we're doing it all the time without knowing it. Our planet Earth is like a dog in a car. The atmosphere around the Earth is like a big glass window. It lets the heat in and it's meant to let the heat out again. But the Earth's ventilation system doesn't work if there's too much carbon dioxide in the atmosphere. Too much carbon dioxide, and the heat – in the form of long-wave radiation – just builds up and builds up, with terrible results. Dogs don't die, but instead the planet itself comes under threat.

The average global surface air temperature has increased by about one degree centigrade in the last hundred and fifty years. Some scientists reckon that a hundred years from now it could have risen by several more degrees. If they're right, the ice-caps will melt, making sea-levels rise, and putting low-level cities – like New York, Tokyo and London – under water. The Thames barrier won't be enough to protect London.

If they're right, there'll be great shifts in climate. They could turn the wheat plains of America and the rice paddy-fields of Asia into gigantic dustbowls, like those parts of drought-stricken Africa today, where we've already seen famine decimate whole nations.

To some extent, scientists can only guess what will happen and how fast it will happen. That's because we're observing a completely new phenomenon. The world's temperature remained stable for millennia, until we started to add more and more carbon dioxide to the atmosphere. We've only been doing that for about a hundred years, since we started to burn larger and larger amounts of fossil fuels to provide heat and power for our industries and our homes.

Fossil fuels – coal, oil and gas – come from inside the Earth. The industries of the Western developed countries burn these fuels in colossal quantities, and now the developing countries are following suit. Many homes use these fuels too, either for heating or for cooking.

Even the electricity we all take for granted is likely to come from a power station which uses fossil fuels. It is possible to make electricity using nuclear energy, but no-one has yet solved the problem of what to do with the radioactive waste products. It's also possible to make electricity using giant windmills or dams and water turbines. But again, these methods have their own problems.

It seems the only sure way we can stop the Earth's temperature rising is by being aware of the problem and being careful with our fossil fuels so that we use less of them.

If you live in a house which has an insulated roof, insulated walls and double-glazing, you're not just saving money, you're saving fossil fuels. If we switch our school heating on a fraction later in the morning and keep the temperature a fraction lower, we'll be saving fossil fuels. If we all watch what we do with electricity – turning off unnecessary lights, not filling a whole kettle when we're only making a mug of coffee – we'll be saving fossil fuels.

It doesn't sound like much, but if everyone does their share, it will make a difference. If we don't make this effort, our grandchildren will wonder why we didn't care about the planet we left to them.

After all, if you could open a car window for a dying dog, you'd do it. *(Pause.)*

RESPONSE

Commitment

With things like global warming it often seems like it's 'someone else's problem' – but it's not. Every person in this hall (*room*) can make a difference. *(Pause.)* The problem is made by millions of us burning fossil fuels directly or indirectly – and it can only be solved by millions of us doing something about it.

If every household in Britain switched off one sixty watt lamp one night, it would save the entire output of one generating station.

■ *Show supplied OHT image.*

The planet we live on is our planet. It doesn't belong to someone else. What happens to it is our responsibility. Let's make a commitment to do something about it in our school and in our own lives at home.

Extra Resources

EEL Energy Efficient Lighting Pack available free to schools with worksheets for KS3 from CREATE.
Tesar, J (1991) *Global Warming*, Blackbirch.
Becklake, J (1989) *The Climate Crisis: Greenhouse effect and ozone layer*, Franklin Watts.
Global Warming – Briefing Sheet No 1, Cambridgeshire County Council, contact Head of Environmental Programme, tel: 01203 317498.

Theme/ Key value

Conservation

Respect for the living environment

Title

Whose is all this junk?

Summary

This assembly uses a short humorous sketch to illustrate the point that waste management is an individual problem.

Resources

Supplied OHT image (p48). Three pre-prepared students to present the sketch. Photocopies of the script. Five plastic carrier bags containing: nine empty drink cans; seven empty food cans; three empty pet food tins; ten empty glass bottles/jars; four kilos of plastic (try old cassette tapes and videos or even a broken portable stereo).

REFLECTION

Did you pick up any litter on your way in this morning? Did you drop any litter?

■ ***Optional*** *Comment about how well the school is doing on the litter front.*

Imagine what school would be like if everyone dropped their litter and no-one picked it up. Think of all the rubbish you put in bins or take home with you. Imagine how much it would add up to in a year. In the UK, the average person throws away ten times their body weight every year. That's quite hard to visualise, so *(names or group)* are going to come and show us.

■ *Two students are Narrator 1 and Narrator 2. The third is Average Person. The sketch should be slick. There's no time for showing and counting every item in each bag as they are mentioned – one example of each will do.*

Narrator 1 This is an average person.

■ *Average Person stands centre.*

Narrator 2 We're going to give him all his junk to carry.

Narrator 1 Nine drink cans.

■ *Lifts out one can to show audience. Gives Average Person the carrier bag with drink cans in.*

Narrator 2 Seven food cans.

■ *As before.*

Narrator 1 Three pet food tins.

Narrator 2 Ten bottles and jars.

Narrator 1 And four kilos of plastic.

■ *Average Person now has five carrier bags.*

Teacher/leader So that's the average person's rubbish for one year?

Narrator 2 No. We couldn't possibly bring everything that should be in the bags, so we divided it all by ten.

Narrator 1 (with emphasis): It should be ninety drinks cans!

■ *Average Person makes that bag seem heavier.*

Narrator 2 And seventy food cans!

■ *Heavier bag as before.*

Narrator 1 Thirty pet food tins!

Narrator 2 One hundred bottles and jars!

Narrator 1 And forty kilos of plastic!

■ *Average Person is now visibly struggling with imagined loads of rubbish.*

Teacher/leader That's the average person's rubbish for one year?

Narrator 2 No. His family also gets through a hundred dustbins of general waste per year.

■ *Average Person very wobbly trying to juggle imagined dustbins.*

pfp, 61 Gray's Inn Road, London WC1X 8TL May be photocopied for use within the purchasing institution only.

Narrator 1 And two trees' worth of waste paper and cardboard.

■ *Average Person collapses on the floor.*

■ *Thank the actors and they can go.*

The real problem with rubbish is knowing what to do with it all. Obviously, we can't carry our own rubbish around all year in carrier bags. So we've got two choices. First, we can throw it all away together – cans, bottles, plastic, paper, all categories in the same bin. However, that way, the rubbish can't be sorted, so it gets buried in big holes in the ground. Eventually it gives off nasty gases in the air and it leeches nasty chemicals into the soil.

The other option is to bin our rubbish in separate containers, either at home or at a recycling point. That way, most of the rubbish can be rescued, processed and used again. Which means we don't have to plunder so much of the Earth's natural resources to make new wood pulp for paper, or to make new metal, glass and plastic.

RESPONSE

Acknowledging failure and shortcomings

■ *Show the supplied OHT image.*

Just for a few moments, let's look at this picture and think of the planet we live on, the planet we depend on. It's easy to blame others for exploiting the Earth and spoiling it – developers who burn away ancient forests, or road builders who cut through natural habitats. But we each carry some responsibility for the state of the Earth. Think of those noxious gases and chemicals coming from the waste tip. *(Pause.)* From my rubbish and yours. *(Pause.)* How many new bottles and cans have had to be made from precious limited resources because we forgot to recycle the old ones? *(Pause.)*

Action

We want our planet to support our children and our grandchildren. We can help to make it happen by the way we deal with our rubbish. Picking up litter is a good way to start.

Extra Resources

Harris, C and Bickerstaf, J (1991) *Waste Management*, Watts.
Taylor, B (1990) *Waste and Recycling*, A&C Black.

Body Shop leaflet, *Reuse, Refill, Recycle*, available from Body Shops. General resources from Friends of the Earth at 26–28 Underwood Street, London N1 7JQ, tel: 0171 490 1555.

Theme/ Key value

Conservation

Respect for the living environment

Title

Junk in space

Summary This assembly introduces the issue of extra-terrestrial pollution in the form of space junk.

Resources Supplied OHT image (p48).

REFLECTION

- *As students assemble, show supplied OHT image.*
- ***Optional** Adapt the first paragraph if you are not using the theme as a whole.*

As we look at the picture which goes with our theme, I'd like you to imagine that you're looking up at the sky, past the trees and away from the Earth. We've been considering the problems that planet Earth has with environmental pollution. We also know that the immediate atmosphere around the Earth is affected by our pollution. But what about space itself? Surely humankind can't spoil space?

Well, the truth is we can, and we have.

Whenever our TV screens show an astronaut on a space-walk outside a spacecraft, we know that these courageous men and women are conquering their fear of technical failure by putting their trust in their lifelines. But there's a much greater fear for the space-walker. That's the fear of being hit by a piece of space junk.

In a world which depends on communications satellites to bring us live pictures for TV news, or whole TV channels via a satellite dish, new satellites are being launched into orbit around the Earth all the time. There are hundreds of these satellites orbiting our planet. Some of them are placed in their correct orbit by the crew of a spacecraft, like the American space shuttle. But most satellites are launched into space attached to rocket launchers. When the launcher separates from its payload, first the connecting bolts are discarded into space, then the rocket itself orbits the Earth as a large piece of junk for several years, before finally exploding into thousands of fragments.

Most of these fragments are too small to be monitored – only space junk measuring ten centimetres can be tracked from Earth. Since the first satellite was launched in 1961, twenty-three thousand bits of measurable space junk have been tracked, some of them very large components like solar panels which have malfunctioned and been ditched. Pieces of space junk shatter into smaller and smaller pieces as they crash into each other at speed. Some pieces leave the Earth's orbit altogether, so there are now about eight thousand measurable bits in orbit.

However, more space junk is added each year at an ever increasing rate. Two hundred and twenty-five new pieces were logged in 1993 and four hundred and fifty in 1994, so it looks as if the numbers could even be doubling, year by year.

Space junk travels at about seventeen thousand miles an hour, depending on which of the Earth's orbits it is in. The closer to the Earth, the faster junk travels. The closer to the Earth, the thicker the layer of junk too, because bits constantly collide and explode into smaller and smaller pieces.

So, as the director of an American watchdog agency put it, 'There's a non-trivial chance that every time an astronaut

© pfp 1998 ISBN 1 874050 39 2

goes out on a space-walk, they're going to get drilled by a wing nut.'

The American shuttle spacecraft return to Earth after launching their satellites, so they leave no debris behind. But they do need a human crew and their safety is often threatened by space junk. On four different flights, shuttle crews have had to manouevre their craft to avoid passing junk. And that's just the big bits.

Every two or three flights, a window which costs thirty thousand pounds has to be replaced because it has been pitted by a tiny paint chip smaller than a flea. But a tiny flaw could cause that window to shatter on the next launch, so safety must come first.

Obviously, we can't turn the clock back and stop using communications satellites. But the question has to be asked – can we just go on and on throwing all our space junk away like this? Polluting the space around our polluted Earth?

The nations which venture into space are being pressed to establish an international treaty. This would rule that all satellite launchers should return to Earth after deploying their satellites. And satellites themselves should carry just enough fuel to bring them back into the Earth's atmosphere after they've become obsolete. Then they would burn up or fall back to Earth, instead of littering the skies above it.

RESPONSE

Expressions of thankfulness

In a moment of quiet, let us be thankful for the world we live in. You might like to look at the picture again. In particular, we can be thankful for the satellites which we can't see in the sky, but which link us up live with all the nations of our world. Satellites which give us TV news, extra TV channel choice and phonecalls to relations on the other side of the planet.

We can be thankful, too, for our awareness of what these benefits are costing our world. Next time there's a debate about the future of television, maybe we'll be the ones who put the hidden factor into the equation. Because we know – all of us – that no-one has the right to leave their space junk in the sky.

Extra Resources

These facts come from an article by Caroline Dopyera in the American newspaper *The News & Observer* (February 10th, 1994).
Tesar, J (1991) *Waste Crisis*, Blackbirch, p18.

Assembly 5 of 5

Conservation

Key Stage 3 and 4

Theme/ Key value

Respect for the living environment

Title

One man's meat...

Summary

This assembly uses interviews with students who are vegetarians to highlight some of the environmental issues which vegetarianism addresses.

Resources

Supplied OHT image (p48). Five or six prepared students who are vegetarians for particular reasons. There can be duplications – it is perhaps preferable that there are – but if at all possible, find students who can between them give nutritional reasons, religious reasons and ethical reasons for their vegetarianism.

REFLECTION

In a school of this size, we all fit into different groups for different purposes. There are the different classes and tutor groups, of course, but apart from those there are the groups who share similar interests.

■ *Adapt the following list to suit your school.*

There are the sports teams *(mention the school's main sports interests)*, the musicians *(mention the choir, the orchestra, jazz band, pop group, etc.)*, the drama enthusiasts *(the school play, for example)*.

Generally speaking, we wouldn't be able to tell just by looking at people which interest group they belonged to. We've got a group of students here this morning who share something in common. But you won't be able to tell what it is just by looking at them.

■ *Bring forward the prepared vegetarians.*

Well, what do you reckon? Singers? Actors? Gymnasts?

■ *Ask the students to introduce themselves one at a time, using this formula: 'My name is..., I'm in class/group... and I'm a vegetarian.'*

■ *Ask one of them to explain what a vegetarian is. The answer should be something like, 'A vegetarian doesn't eat meat or fish, and some don't eat eggs or dairy products either.'*

■ *Now ask each of them in turn to give their reasons for eating a vegetarian diet.*

You probably noticed that we've got different reasons here for being a vegetarian. *(Name)* is a vegetarian *(or 'some people are vegetarians')* for nutritional reasons. The modern Western diet, which is high in animal fat and low in vegetable fibre, is now thought to be unhealthy. Many people now eat a healthy alternative diet of naturally-grown vegetables, fruits and grains, trying to avoid food that has been chemically treated or over-processed.

(Name) is a vegetarian *(or 'some people are vegetarians')* for religious reasons. Vegetarianism seems to have started as a religious practice about three thousand years ago, a way of purifying the body as an aid to purifying the soul. Some Muslims today – the Sufi mystics – recommend a vegetarian diet for spiritual seekers. And some Jews and Christians *(like name)* also observe strict vegetarian guidelines.

Some Hindus and some Buddhists practise vegetarianism for a different religious reason. They believe *(like name)* that all animal life is sacred and that humans should avoid harming animals in any way.

(Name) is a vegetarian *(or 'some people are vegetarians')* for ethical rather than strictly religious reasons. Many people today believe it is wrong to exploit the animal

kingdom for food when a vegetarian diet can provide adequate nutrition for humans.

Others avoid eating meat simply because of the way the animals are treated. In order to get the best return for their investment, many animal farmers feed their stock with inappropriate food just to make them fatter and fatter, and they automatically give them antibiotics to prevent them getting ill.

The animals are often kept in conditions which are convenient to the meat-producer, but which are unnatural for the animal. You may know about the crates used for raising veal calves in some European countries – though these have in fact been banned in the UK for some years.

And no matter how humane the killing system in our abattoirs, many people reject the idea of raising animals just in order to kill them for food. Some would also say that converting animal grazing land to crop-growing land would make more food available to the world as a whole, anyway.

It is a sad fact that for some of the poorer developing countries, meat has become a valuable export commodity. Instead of growing traditional crops, farmers now raise cattle to export to richer developed countries. In parts of South America, huge tracts of forests are being burned away to make new grazing land for export beef.

When your parents were at school, there weren't many vegetarians. In some schools it would have been difficult to find anyone to come and talk to an assembly about their reasons for choosing a vegetarian diet. When your parents were young, vegetarians were often thought of as cranks and weirdos. Today, as we have experienced here this morning, vegetarians are more likely to be seen as thoughtful, caring, even religious people.

RESPONSE

Celebration

In a moment of quiet, let us think first of all about the great diversity of ideas and interests we have here in our school. We're not all sports enthusiasts, musicians or performers. We're not all vegetarians. But we do all recognise that the tolerance we have and the encouragement we give each other to follow particular beliefs and interests is part of what makes our school a good place to be. If you believe in God, you might like to express your positive feelings about our school in a silent prayer. *(Pause.)*

Commitment

■ *Show supplied OHT image.*

We've seen this morning that our choices about what we eat can affect our own health. They can also affect the health of our planet and its animals. We may not all agree with vegetarians, but they remind us that we have responsibilities to all living things. They stress the importance of humane farming and if we think carefully about the way food is produced and make those values clear when we buy our food, we can influence farmers and retailers. (*Pause.*) Remember, we're not owners of our planet – we're here for a short time and can only care and look after our world for future generations.

Extra Resources

Lobstein, T and Dibb, S (1991) *At the Take-away*, Wayland (part of the Food Production series).

Theme

Choice and decisions

Assemblies on this theme

1 **What makes you choose?**
This assembly looks at some real-life choices and the values behind them.

2 **Dietrich Bonhoeffer**
This assembly uses the story of Dietrich Bonhoeffer as an encouragement to choose right against wrong.

3 **Learning to compromise**
This assembly uses some contemporary case histories to encourage students to recognise that some decisions require compromise and that it's not always a direct choice between saying 'yes' or 'no'.

4 **Moral dilemmas: How do you choose? (Abortion)**
This assembly uses the debate around the issue of abortion to look very complex decisions and how such dilemmas deserve much thought before choosing a perspective.

5 **Democracy**
This assembly challenges students to exercise their democratic right to vote. when they are 18.

Record of use

Taken by	1	2	3	4	5
Date					
Given to					

Comments

pfp, 61 Gray's Inn Road, London WC1X 8TL May be photocopied for use within the purchasing institution only.

pfp, 61 Gray's Inn Road, London WC1X 8TL May be photocopied for use within the purchasing institution only.
 ISBN 1 874050 39 2

Theme/ Key value

Choice and decisions

Striving for personal development and a sense of moral autonomy

Title

What makes you choose?

Summary

This assembly looks at some real-life choices and the values behind them. **WARNING!** Make sure there are no relatives or friends present of those involved before delivering the assembly.

Resources

A student to read the newsreports.

REFLECTION

How many of you have ever really thought about the choices and decisions you have to make? Making choices and decisions is part of being human. We've all made several already today. What time to get up, what to wear, what to eat... Most of the time, we make decisions like these without much thought, because they're not huge, life-changing decisions. Having said that, the time it takes many of us to choose what to wear when we're going somewhere special, you'd think it was a matter of life and death! But, on the whole, those sorts of decisions are not things we spend a lot of time thinking about.

■ ***Optional*** *Adapt the following paragraph if you are not using the theme as a whole.*

Over the next few assemblies, we *are* going to be thinking about choices and decisions. We'll consider some careful choices made with a lot of thought and some which have been made in a split second. But they'll all be important as seeing other people's choices will help us to understand some of the reasons behind the decisions we make.

We're going to start with a story that was in the news during a spell of very cold weather. As you listen, think about the reasons for the decisions being made. *(Name of reader)* will be our newsreader.

Reader: The parents of a girl who drowned in a frozen lake recently, paid tribute yesterday to the two men who also died in their attempts to rescue her. Tracey Pattison, aged eleven, died after following a dog onto thin ice at Hemsworth Water Park thirteen days ago. Michael Mee, aged forty-eight, an off-duty fireman, and Jack Crawshaw, aged fifty-one, a retired grocer, tried to save her but fell into the water when the ice collapsed under their weight.

Teresa and Derek Pattison said in a statement: 'Our thoughts go out to Michael and Jack's families. These two men tried to help Tracey, sparing no thought for their own safety. Tracey was a happy, fun-loving eleven-year-old who everybody knew and liked. She was a devoted animal lover and it does not surprise us that she tried to save the dog that fell through the ice. She would have acted on instinct and not thought of the dangers.'

■ *Thank the reader.*

Tracey made the choice to try to rescue the dog without stopping to think about it first. What do you think made her do it? *(Pause)* Her parents said she was an animal lover. She had probably been brought up that way – to be caring to animals, to help them if they were in distress, to see that even an animal's life is very precious. Because of these values, her instinct was to save the dog. This was combined with the fact that she was young and inexperienced, and probably wasn't fully aware of the dangers of running onto the ice, of the risk she was taking.

But what about the men who tried to save her? They chose to take that risk. What do you think made them make that split-second decision, rather than looking after themselves? They were a lot older than Tracey and knew the dangers.

Michael and Jack made a decision based on values that were supremely important to them. Those values included counting a child's life as important, and meant that they were prepared to take the risk in order to save her life. They didn't have time to think about their values before deciding what to do – they had to make a split-second decision. But that decision was still controlled by the values they held. Those values were so strong that they guided their instincts. *(Pause)*

As you get older, you'll be faced with a growing number of more difficult or more complicated decisions than those you had to make when you were children. And some will be moral decisions, in which you can make wise or unwise choices.

Let's think of some examples for a moment – you may have faced some of them already. For example, do you start to smoke cigarettes, or not? *(Pause)* If you know someone has been stealing, do you report them, or not? Do you take notice of the warnings about drugs like ecstasy, and tragedies like Leah Betts, or not? Do you spend extra time studying for a while to make sure you pass your exams, or not?

Why do you think some people make unwise choices when they are faced with decisions like this? If the option is between something which is good for them and something which isn't, why do some people choose the one which isn't?

Well, sometimes it's because they don't know enough to actually calculate the risks and so they make a mistake – like Tracey not being fully aware of the dangers of ice. But often it's because they make split-second decisions, without having thought about their values and beliefs beforehand. If you know what you value, your instincts will be guided by those values, and you're much more likely to make a wise quick decision than an unwise one.

Some take a cigarette because everyone else has, or they don't study because they don't want to be known as a 'swot'. At the time, the desire to be 'cool' is often a lot more important than the risks involved in taking drugs or not bothering to get qualifications. That's understandable – it's important to most people to be able to fit in with their chosen group of friends.

But some choices you have *are* important, and we don't often have to make quick decisions about them. They're so important that it's worth taking time and care to make sure you make the right one. What do you really think about it? Is your decision going to harm you in any way? Smoking will, of course, and so will wasting your education. Will it harm other people? Rushed decisions may well cause hurt to others, even if you don't mean it. Does it fit in with the values that you have – caring for and respecting yourself and others?

RESPONSE

Action

Here in school, there are choices to be made. Some of the day-to-day decisions you make will be instinctive. But perhaps we should all try to be more thoughtful about our choices and decisions when we can – thinking about the values which determine our actions. Doing the best we can, joining in and playing our part are all values that we rate as important. They are areas in which we can choose whether or not to contribute to the life of the school community for the benefit of all. They are moral decisions.

Commitment

Whatever decisions we make – whether in our school or personal lives – let's resolve to give thought to them whenever we can, and to make sure that they're not based on selfishness, but on worthwhile values. Values such as caring *(Pause)*, sacrifice *(Pause)* and good sense. *(Pause)*

Theme/ Key value

Choice and decisions

Striving for personal development and a sense of moral autonomy

Title

Dietrich Bonhoeffer

Summary

This assembly uses the story of Dietrich Bonhoeffer as an encouragement to choose right against wrong.

Resources

There are no resources needed for this assembly.

REFLECTION

■ ***Optional*** *Adapt the following paragraph if you are not using the theme as a whole.*

The theme we've been thinking about is choices and decisions. I wonder what's the hardest decision you've ever had to make? *(Pause)* Sometimes a decision is hard because the choices offered to you are equally attractive. For example, there are two films you want to see and they're on on the same night, for that night only.

And then other decisions are hard to make because of what the result might be. You might want to demonstrate against felling trees to build a motorway, but you're worried that if there's trouble you could end up being injured or arrested. You have to choose between how you feel about the threat to the environment compared with how you feel about the worry your parents would have for you.

And sometimes a decision is hard because it might mark you out as different. Some people who choose to be faithful to their religion, for example, may face hostility if they have to wear special clothes or abstain from things like alcohol.

But imagine if your decision could cost you your life. Listen to this true story for the next couple of minutes and consider the difficulty of the choices and decisions that the man involved had to make.

❝In the 1930s in Germany, Dietrich Bonhoeffer was a minister in the German Protestant Church. It was the time when Germany was ruled by the National Socialist Party – the Nazis – and throughout the country many members of the Church sympathised with the Nazi campaign for what they called the 'moral re-birth' of Germany. But Bonhoeffer had no such sympathies. He knew they were mistaken and that the Nazi belief in the supremacy of the German race above all others was immoral. Many other German people agreed with him, but to stand up for these beliefs against the ruling party was a dangerous and rare act. The Nazis had no respect for democracy – as we now know, they were willing to exterminate any person or group which posed a challenge or threat to their goal.

But Bonhoeffer's own beliefs and values were so strong that it was impossible for him to accept what the Nazis were doing in his country. In 1934, he made the first of many brave decisions. Together with a group of like-minded people, he openly set up a new group called the Confessing Church, including a college to train the group's ministers. To choose to publicly form a group in opposition to the Nazi party was dangerous and brave.

Of course, it didn't go unnoticed. Bonhoeffer must have felt the weight of hatred against him. It would have been much easier for him quietly to continue working in the mainstream Church. But he couldn't, and he chose to go on with his act of opposition.

Three years later, the college was declared illegal by the Nazis, but Bonhoeffer chose to ignore the ban. He also realised that Christians around the world could unite to oppose the Nazi evil and he began to lecture about it in the UK and the USA, even before the Second World War started in 1939. He was in the USA when it became clear what the Nazi government was going to do. His friends there tried to persuade him to stay with them, in safety. He knew that he could be risking his life by returning, but he was a patriot and believed that he should be in his own country at such a time, doing what he could for the cause of truth. He knew he must share the horrors of Nazi rule with his fellow Christians in his home country. Again, it was a brave and difficult choice. He took the last ship from the USA to Germany before the War broke out.

There were, of course, others who were actively resistant to Hitler's rule, and they began to work together. With his contacts outside Germany, Bonhoeffer became a vital link between the German resistance and the outside world. Again, imagine the courage it must have taken to choose to work in this way. In effect, he was an undercover spy. How many of us would risk this danger and the near certainty of death if we were caught?

(Pause) And disaster did strike. In April 1943, Dietrich Bonhoeffer was arrested by the Nazi secret police – the Gestapo. He was kept in prison until a year later, when the Gestapo found documents linking him with other conspirators and moved him to a concentration camp. But all the while, he carried on praying for peace, and although he could no longer actively oppose the Nazis, this and his own inner peace was an inspiration to other prisoners. One of them said later, 'He even won over his guards. He said to me over and over again that the only fight we lose is the one we give up.'

In April 1945, together with others who had opposed the party, Dietrich Bonhoeffer was executed at the concentration camp at Flossenburg. It was Hitler's final act of revenge, before taking his own life. The German minister went to his death as bravely as he had lived, kneeling first to pray in the morning sunshine. Only a few days later, the camp was liberated by American troops.” *(Pause)*

We live in a democratic country, which means that we are free to speak out against the government if we disagree with them, and we are given a chance to vote for who we do agree with every four years or so. In other words, we have a choice. And, of course, Germany is now the same. But there are still some countries where going against the authorities is one of the hardest choices you can make, and where people continue to choose to risk their lives by doing so.

RESPONSE

Commitment and action

Fortunately, because we are lucky enough to live in a democratic country, few of us here will ever be in a situation like Dietrich Bonhoeffer was. But, sometimes, we will still have to make big decisions – decisions which require moral courage, decisions which involve our fundamental beliefs, where we feel that we have to stand up for what we think is right.

Perhaps you're faced with someone being bullied because of their race or religion for example – something you know is wrong. What do you do?

On these occasions, perhaps we will remember Dietrich Bonhoeffer and learn from his story. May his example give us the courage to make the same choice – to stand up for our beliefs – in our own circumstances, whatever they are. *(Pause)*

Theme/ Key value

Choice and decisions

Striving for personal development and a sense of moral autonomy

Title

Learning to compromise

Summary

This assembly uses some contemporary case histories to encourage students to recognise that some decisions require compromise and that it's not always a direct choice between saying 'yes' or 'no'.

Resources

There are no resources needed for this assembly.

REFLECTION

When you think about it, there are numerous different kinds of decisions that we have to make. Some are more complicated than others. Some, for example, don't really matter very much. Shall I play some music or watch TV? Shall I have beans or soup? It all depends on your preference. Or perhaps there is a clear and sensible 'yes' or 'no' answer. Should I wear my winter coat on a hot and sunny day in August? Well, you'd be a bit silly if you did, but it still doesn't really matter. We have to make these everyday decisions, but they make very little difference to how we grow and develop as people.

Then there are those decisions which you know *are* important. Perhaps where your choice is between two things rather more significant than a tin of beans and a tin of soup. Shall I stay on at school or leave, for example? Or where the obvious answer is also the most difficult one. Shall I start to smoke cigarettes like all my friends do? Decisions which can change your life.

But many decisions offer neither clear choices nor clear answers, and these are sometimes the hardest decisions to make. In these cases, there's often a need to find the best solution rather than the right answer – a need to find a compromise.

Some people think that compromising is a 'cop out' – that being strong means you can make a decision and stick to it, regardless of what the decision is. And in some cases they're right. It may be hard not to give in to the temptation of smoking if all your friends do, for example. But if you can continue to resist it, you must be a strong person.

But that's not always the case. Sometimes being strong means that you are prepared to think problems through clearly, with an open mind. That you are prepared to think of everyone involved, think of the long-term consequences of the decision, and find the solution that perhaps isn't exactly right, but which suits everyone in the best possible way it can.

Let's consider a few such problems. Imagine for a moment that you are helping a friend to decide whether to say 'yes', 'no', or whether to find a 'best' solution. What do you think should happen in these situations?

Here's the first one. Your friend Roxanne is fifteen and has been your friend since you started at this school. Recently, you met a new friend and you're really enjoying yourself with her crowd. You seem to be accepted and fit in easily. They laugh at your jokes, they have similar tastes to you and you look forward to weekends when you'll go around together.

One problem, though. They're not keen on Roxanne. She's not their sort and although you've been good mates for a few years now, you feel you've grown apart a bit. She tells you she feels left out and wants to know why you aren't around at weekends like you used to be. She's been a good friend and you feel a bit guilty but you want to be part of the other group.

What should you do? What do you say to Roxanne and your new friends? Is there a compromise solution? *(Pause)*

Here's another one. You've got a friend called Paul. He's into boxing and likes to show off sometimes. Paul's thirteen and has a younger brother called Matt who's eleven. Matt's not into boxing. He was in a car crash once and now he's got a permanent limp. Paul's really mad because he's just found out that a couple of bullies have been taking money from Matt and threatening him because of his limp. He tells you that he's going to sort them out after school – blood will flow. Paul's sometimes on a short fuse and you know his reaction is only going to lead to trouble for everyone. But Matt needs protecting. What should Paul do? Is there a compromise solution? *(Pause)* What would you say to Paul? *(Pause)*

Here's the last one. You've got a friend called Craig who's fifteen. Craig has a cousin called Damien who's a bit older and ill with a rare form of cancer. Damien's not confined to bed, but he can't do much because he tires very easily. They get on well and Craig often goes round to sit with him – they play CDs or watch TV or videos. Craig's promised to go round next Friday night with some new CDs. But he'd forgotten that he'd been invited to a great party that Friday at a mate's house to celebrate his brother's eighteenth birthday. And obviously that's a one-off – he's never going to be eighteen again. Is there a compromise solution? *(Pause)* What would you say to Craig? *(Pause)*

RESPONSE

Well, we've heard three case histories – three situations in which people are having to make difficult choices.

Should you just leave Roxanne? How would you really feel if you did that? How do you think Roxanne would feel? Suppose your new friends turn out to be a bit boring after a while. *(Pause)* What can you do? What choices are open to you?

Should Paul beat up the lads who are tormenting his brother? The emotional answer might be 'yes!', but he would be getting himself into trouble. He might get hurt. He might only make the bullies worse. And would it be right for him to stoop to their level, behaving just like they are? We know that violence doesn't actually solve anything. So we know that the answer is 'no'. But then that wouldn't make them stop, would it? So perhaps you'll have to think of an additional option. Perhaps he could try to talk to them, with you as support. Perhaps… well you think how he could solve the problem.

And what about Craig? Should he go to the party or to Damien's? He'll have to think about Damien's feelings and his relationship with him in the future. Maybe he'll have to think about how ill he is at that time. Perhaps there's a way in which he could do both – explain the situation to Damien, go round there a bit earlier and go on to the party later. What would you do?

Commitment

Many of our choices are not a straight decision between two courses of action. But sometimes it takes more effort to find a compromise than to make a quick decision, so we don't bother. But compromise is a great skill to learn and to have. Next time you have a difficult decision to make, try to think through all the possibilities and come up with something that lets you feel good about what you've decided and shows some care and concern for other people too.

Remember, sometimes you need to say 'How can I compromise and still do the right thing?' It's not always black and white.

Theme/ Key value

Choice and decisions

Striving for personal development and a sense of moral autonomy

Title

Moral dilemmas: How do you choose? (Abortion)

Summary This assembly uses the debate around the issue of abortion to look very complex decisions and how such dilemmas deserve much thought before choosing a perspective. **WARNING!** This is a deliberately non-judgmental discussion of a very sensitive issue which you may not feel is suitable for your school or group, or which you may prefer to use as a tutorial with a particular group of students. Please read it carefully before using it.

Resources Two students (good readers) to act out the debate.

REFLECTION

■ ***Optional*** *Adapt the following paragraph if you are not using the theme as a whole.*

We've been thinking about choices and decisions. Today we're going to consider an example of one of the hardest types of decisions people have to make – what we could call a moral dilemma. Moral dilemmas are usually situations in which there is a choice to be made between two perspectives. Many people have strong feelings about them. The decision you usually have to make is which side you agree with, according to your personal beliefs and priorities. These situations often need a number of choices to be made before you reach your final decision, so they deserve real thought – they're not choices to be taken lightly.

This particular example has been backed by law, challenged by fierce demonstrations and continues to be fervently debated throughout the world. The choice we're talking about is deciding whether or not to have an abortion. *(Pause)* Let's think carefully about the different perspectives we can choose from. *(Name of Reader 1)*, you're representing some of those who disagree with abortion.

Reader 1: I have a firm religious faith. My faith has taught me that life is sacred and God-given and shouldn't be taken away. But science has also taught me that even before a woman knows she is pregnant, the foetus is a living organism with its own heart and blood and whose eyes, spinal cord, nervous system and main organs are already beginning to form. I firmly believe that this is human life, which begins at the moment of conception. So an abortion is actually the taking of a life – murder, if you like.

That sounds like a good argument. *(Name of Reader 2)*, you're representing some of those who agree with abortion. What do you say to that?

Reader 2: Well, although the foetus begins to develop its own features from the point of conception, it's not able to survive without its mother until it's about twenty-four weeks old. I believe that it's at this point – when it's no longer totally dependent on the mother's body for survival – that human life begins. Until then, I believe that every woman has the right to choose what happens to her body.

(Sound surprised and confused.) Oh! Well, that's a good argument too. So there's one choice we have to make before we decide. Okay, let's hear some of the other points.

Reader 2: Abortion is a traumatic experience. But, in the long term for some women, it may be less traumatic than the experience of giving birth and being responsible for a child. What if the baby was a result of rape? Or if the mother is so young she wouldn't realistically be able to look after a baby?

Reader 1: You're right, in some cases pregnancy and childbirth are particularly difficult. But abortion is *very* traumatic. It can leave deep and long-lasting physical and

 ISBN 1 874050 39 2

mental scars. I think you underestimate this – and that many women don't realise it when they choose to have an abortion. In some cases it can leave the woman unable to have children.

Not having an abortion doesn't mean keeping the child. The baby can be adopted. There are many more childless couples desperate for a child to love than there are children to adopt, so he or she would be sure to go to a good and caring home.

Reader 2: But then having to give away her baby after giving birth to it may leave more mental scars on the mother than having an early abortion. And not all people do give their child up for adoption – many do keep them, even if they don't really want them or are not really able to look after them.

And what if the child is going to be severely handicapped? This can make it much harder for him or her to be adopted, and abortion gives parents the chance to decide at an early stage whether they can cope with the extra responsibility of a disabled child.

Reader 1: But this could mean that many disabled children are needlessly aborted. Many people assume that disabled people are abnormal or useless, but most disabled people live perfectly happy and creative lives – everyone has a right to that opportunity.

Did you know that the UN Declaration of the Rights of the Child – which many countries, including the UK, have promised to abide by – states that children need protection before, as well as after, birth?

Reader 2: Hmm. Well I have a different perspective on what that means. Abortion may be fairer than bringing a child into poverty, for example, or perhaps homelessness or neglect. It may be better than knowing that it is unwanted and unloved – every child has the right to feel wanted and loved.

Also, stopping abortions being available wouldn't stop unwanted pregnancies. And that would mean a return to the days of illegal abortions, where anyone could charge a fortune to desperate women. This can be very dangerous – these people often don't know what they're doing, and can even cause the death of the pregnant woman.

Reader 1: But if we had decent education and people took more care of what they did – for example, choosing to have sex when they know that the baby which might result would be wanted and cared for, for example – then abortion wouldn't be necessary at all.

Phew! Okay, hold it there.

Reader 2: But there are other things too...

Reader 1: Yes, and from my point of view...

Yes, I'm sure, but I'm we can't take in much more at the moment!

RESPONSE

Commitment

I wonder what you're all thinking now. Do you know which perspective you agree with? Maybe your faith has taught you the same as *(name of Reader 1)*. Perhaps you're confused and not sure what to think.

But I hope you can see how difficult some decisions and choices are. And how when they're that difficult, it's worth finding out as much as you can about the different perspectives before you make up your mind. Giving careful thought to issues like this is only fair and right. Often, they involve other people – here a foetus or a child – and they deserve you to respect them by not rushing into making badly thought-out decisions. But also it's fair to yourself to think about it carefully because then, whatever you decide in the end, you can be sure of your choice, and you're less likely to end up feeling hurt, or having to live with a situation that you will regret for a long time to come.

Extra Resources

Titner, M (1989) *State Imperfect – The Book of Social Problems*. London: Optima. **The Society for the Protection of Unborn Children**, 7 Tufton Street, London SW1P 3QN. **The Brook Advisory Centres**, 165 Gray's Inn Road, London WC1X 8UD. **Education for Choice**, 11–13 Charlotte Street, London W1P 1HD.

Theme/ Key value

Choice and decisions

Striving for personal development and a sense of moral autonomy

Title

Democracy

Summary

This assembly challenges students to exercise their democratic right to vote when they are eighteen.

Resources

Supplied OHT image (p60).

REFLECTION

Before we do anything else, I need to hold a vote this morning. We're thinking about making all PE lessons for the rest of this year cross-country *(or another sport that is relatively unpopular in your school)* only. Could I have a show of hands from those in favour? Just a few. Oh well, sorry you lot, but it looks like it's business as usual.

What we've just seen is a simple demonstration of democracy at work. Much more basic than the complicated systems countries need in order to run democratically of course, but the principles are pretty much the same. Everyone had the chance to vote and the minority, who were outvoted, now have to live by the decision of the majority.

Now if I was going to be undemocratic, I could have just asked a few select people, in private, to choose what we should all do. But then I'm sure many of you, quite rightly, would have complained. You'd have said, 'Sir/Miss, that's not fair. You should have asked everybody!'

Another way I could have done it would have been to put a notice up, asking everyone to hand in a slip at the office with their vote on it. I would be trying to be democratic, because I would be giving everyone the opportunity to have their say. But how many people do you think would vote? Quite possibly only those who had very strong feelings either way. But if the majority of those who did vote wanted to do cross-country only, everyone would have to do it. And how many people who didn't vote do you think would suddenly find that they did feel strongly about it? I'm sure there would be a fair few complaints then! They'd say it was unfair – but would it be? Can it be unfair if you've chosen not to take part?

You will all be able to vote in local and national elections in a few years. Once you're eighteen, it's your right to choose the candidate you think is best for the job. You can do that because we live in a democracy. 'Democracy' means 'government by the people' – everyone has the right to take part in decisions about how their community is run. But it would be impractical to get everyone in a country to vote on every single issue, so most modern democracies hold elections where the people choose candidates to represent them in a Parliament. These elected representatives then vote on behalf of the people who chose them.

The trouble with leaving the decision-making to a few hundred professionals, though, is that the ordinary people can start to lose interest. Or they become disillusioned when there are too many decisions made that they don't agree with. The end result is that people stop bothering to vote in elections to choose their representatives.

But if democracy is truly to be government by the people, it should really be by *all* the people. If some people don't vote, it's not really democratic. For democracy to work, as many people as possible need to vote so that when laws are made in Parliament, they are made by candidates who represent all the people, not just some of them.

Not all countries are democratic. Around the world, there continue to be places where laws are imposed on everyone by a single dictator or a repressive military dictatorship. Until 1990, South Africa was undemocratic – only the white minority were allowed to vote. But the freedom to voice your opinion through a vote is such a great right that people like Nelson Mandela, imprisoned for twenty-five years, and Steve Biko, who died in police custody, risked their lives fighting for it.

In the UK, everyone over eighteen can vote, but evidence shows that most young voters just don't bother. A common feeling is that 'my little vote won't make any difference'. But imagine if everyone who said that did vote. All of those single votes added together would make a much bigger one – and that could make a difference.

Another common feeling is that 'the politicians aren't interested in what I want anyway'. And you may or may not be right! But the decisions they make still affect you, and apathy can be a dangerous thing. Apathetic people are a dream come true for tyrants who want everything to happen in their own interests. If you don't bother to vote, they don't have to take your interests into account. And also, of course, if you don't vote, you've no chance of getting the people who *might* be interested! If enough young people don't bother, the people who are elected will be those who only represent the views of older people and who take little account of the opinions and experiences of young people. Do you think that the young people who don't vote then have a right to complain about that? Well, not really, because they haven't tried to make it different.

■ ***Optional*** *Adapt the following paragraph as necessary.*

Now, what would you say is the biggest interest – perhaps the biggest influence – in most young people's lives? Not politics, obviously. Music? Probably. That's why some people in the UK music business have set up a campaign called 'Rock the Vote'. The idea is that they might be able to persuade young people over eighteen to get out and use their vote in elections.

The campaign is backed by bands, record companies, clubs and all the main political parties – despite the fact that thousands of new young voters could also rock their boats! But they are backing it because they know that to make the most of the great freedom we have of living in a democracy, as many people as possible have to exercise their right to vote.

RESPONSE

Expressions of thankfulness

How you vote when you are eighteen depends entirely on your assessment of which candidates live up to your personal ideals. But whether to vote is the first decision you have to make. Remember, if you don't bother to play your part, you can't really complain about the way the country's run.

■ *Show supplied OHT image.*

You have the democratic right not to vote, but if you're just not bothered, think for a moment of all the people around the world who don't even have the right, and be thankful that you do have that privilege.

Commitment

Perhaps you'll also remember these words from Abraham Lincoln, who was President of the United States in the 1860s: 'No man is good enough to govern another man without that other's consent.'
Think about that. It may be a few years away before you can give your consent, but you can resolve now to do so.

Extra Resources

The quote from Abraham Lincoln comes from a speech of 16 October 1854, the first of the Lincoln Douglas Debates. It can be found in *The Columbia Dictionary of Quotations* Columbia University Press.

Theme

What's it worth?

Assemblies on this theme

1 What am I bid?
This assembly introduces the theme by using a mock auction to help students reflect on the nature of value. It highlights the difference between financial and personal value and helps students recognise that most values are personal. It needs some preparation.

2 They were only coins
This assembly sets out to help students reflect on the choices which values present and the idea of a powerful value being linked emotionally to objects. It is followed by an extract from a contemporary novel illustrating a teenager finding that there are values other than those of the market and that these can be stronger and carry greater meaning.

3 Bin it and buy a new one?
This assembly uses a story to show that carelessness towards possessions can be destructive and wasteful and that a sense of personal responsibility can have positive environmental effects.

4 The wrong trainers
This assembly uses a dialogue to help students reflect on the way in which material values, the media, and peer group pressure can contrive to manipulate or influence our value judgements.

5 Real riches
This assembly uses the story of Jean Paul Getty to help the students to consider what is of real value to them.

Record of use

Taken by	1	2	3	4	5
Date					
Given to					

Comments

pfp, 61 Gray's Inn Road, London WC1X 8TL ISBN 1 874050 39 2

WHAT'S IT WORTH? • OHT

 ISBN 1 874050 39 2

Theme/ Key value

What's it worth? Sense of personal responsibility

Title

What am I bid?

Summary

This assembly introduces the theme by using a mock auction to help students reflect on the nature of value. It highlights the difference between financial and personal value and helps students recognise that most values are personal. It needs some preparation.

Resources

Supplied OHT image (p72). Plastic carrier bag containing a ring in a box, an item of sports equipment (see below), a used copy of *The Complete Works of Shakespeare*, a bottle of perfume and a loaf of bread. The sports equipment should be something which could have been used by someone famous, eg. a champion's tennis racket. The text uses goalkeeper's gloves – adapt it according to the item you use. Twelve students to be bidders in the 'auction'.

REFLECTION

I wonder, have you ever been to an auction? You know, where there are lots of items for sale and they display them one by one and ask people to make bids for them, and the highest bidder gets the item. At a cattle market, the auctioneer rattles through the rising bids so fast it sounds like a foreign language. But sometimes on television you see priceless treasures being auctioned. It's all very quiet, the bids go up £1,000 a time and the auctioneer leaves lots of pauses in case someone else wants to put in a higher bid.

Well, we're not exactly having an auction here this morning, because you probably haven't got the odd thousand or two tucked down your sock! But we're going to do something similar. I've asked a group of you to help me with our auction.

- *Bring up a group of about twelve students to act as bidders.*

I'm going to show you three items, and I want you to give me some idea of what you think each item is worth. I'll start the bidding each time, and if you think the item is worth more than I say, put your hand up and I'll take higher bids.

- ***Optional*** *If you have a small assembly group you could use all the students present as the auction participants.*

Right, first item.

- *Take out the ring box from the carrier bag, open it in full view of the students, remove the ring and hold it up.*

This is a lady's ring made of twenty-two carat gold and set with three diamonds *(or appropriate description)*. It could be an engagement ring, and I'd say it's worth about £200. Any higher estimates than that? What do you think it's worth?

- *Take higher bids, but not too many.*

Actually, I'd quite like to sell this ring. If anyone's interested you can see me at break, but I need to know how many are genuinely interested. Put your hand up if you're prepared to pay *(quote highest bid)* for this ring.

- *You shouldn't get any takers, but if you do, make it seem as if there are too few to be bothered with.*

Well, we all seem to agree that the ring is pretty valuable, but we're not exactly falling over ourselves to buy it. I'd better put it safely back in its box.

- *Return the ring box to the carrier bag.*

Item two.

- *Take the 'famous' sports item from the carrier bag and adapt the following text to suit the item and any current major sporting event.*

Now this is *(a pair of goal-keeper's gloves or whatever)*. If I were to tell you that these

 ISBN 1 874050 39 2

(are the gloves that David Seaman wore in every game in Euro '96 or whatever is appropriate) what would they be worth? £10? £20? What would you pay for *(this/them)* if they were on offer?

■ *Take bids, but not too many.*

No, I think I can get more from some really serious fans.

■ *Return the gloves to the bag.*

Okay – last item.

■ *Take the* Complete Shakespeare *from the carrier bag.*

The Complete Works of William Shakespeare. Second-hand copy. Shall we say £40?

■ *Be ready for derisory response!*

£20 then?

■ *More derision.*

£10? £9?

■ *Count down until someone risks a bid.*

It seems that Mr Shakespeare is not in the same league as a sporting treasure or a diamond ring when it comes to value.

But let's change the scenario for a moment. Let's say you want a career on the stage and you've got a provisional place at a drama school, but you've got to pass an audition to get in. It's the night before the audition and you have to be word-perfect on a passage from *Macbeth* – you need to know your Shakespeare.

You've done a fair bit of preparation but you still need to practise. You've left that till the last night so everything will be fresh in your head in the morning. But now – you can't find the book, your *Complete Works of William Shakespeare*. It's not in your bag, it's not on your bed, or under it, or anywhere. School is locked. The public library is closed. What do you do? *(Pause)* You reduce the house to a bomb-site, then you phone a friend who you know has got a Shakespeare. 'Sure!' says your friend. 'You can have my Shakespeare. But it'll cost you!'

■ *Hold up the book again.*

What would you pay for this book now? £5? £10? Remember, your career as a brilliant TV and film actor depends on this audition!

■ *Show supplied OHT image.*

Value is a funny thing. It's not the same as price. There is a high price on a diamond ring in a shop. But what about the value of a cheap ring that was bought for you by someone you really love? If that was stolen, you'd give much more to get it back than the few pounds it cost originally.

The shop price for a champion's sports gear might be a lot less than the value a fan would put on owning it. And a tatty book can be the most valuable thing in your house – the night before an important audition.

RESPONSE

Action

■ *Take the perfume and loaf of bread from the carrier bag.*

Which is worth more – the perfume or the bread? *(Pause)* This perfume cost about £20. The bread about 60 pence. In a *(Ethiopian, or appropriate location in the news where food supply is an issue)* street market today you'd get no takers for the perfume. *(Pause)* You'd get £20 for the bread.

■ *Return the perfume to the bag, but leave the bread on view. Then pause.*

When you're really up against it, what do you value? Do diamonds and expensive cars really matter? It's important to remind ourselves what is really important so that we can keep a sense of perspective. Perhaps this can help us be happier and more at one with ourselves, not confusing the price of something with its value. Jesus said, 'Where your heart is, there will your treasure be also.' *(Pause)*

Extra Resources

The words of Jesus are from the Revised Standard Version of the Bible, Matthew, Chapter 6, verse 21.

 ISBN 1 874050 39 2

Theme/ Key value

What's it worth?

Sense of personal responsibility

Title

They were only coins

Summary

This assembly sets out to help students reflect on the choices which values present and the idea of a powerful value being linked emotionally to objects. It is followed by an extract from a contemporary novel illustrating a teenager finding that there are values other than those of the market and that these can be stronger and carry greater meaning.

Resources

Two prepared members of staff, each with an item of personal value to show and talk about very briefly.

REFLECTION

I've asked a couple of members of staff to bring something to show us this morning. *(Names of members of staff)* are each going to show us something which is really special to them and tell us why it's so special.

- *Introduce the members of staff in turn and let them explain briefly why their item is special. When they have both spoken, thank them.*

The thing I noticed about those particular treasures was that their true value wasn't measured in in terms of money but in what they stood for. They had a personal value for their owners. That's what made them special.

Here's an extract from a novel. It's an incident where someone discovers that kind of value. The story is set in America and the central character is a teenage boy called Chappie who recalls a time when he desperately needed some money and went searching the house for something he could sell. He finds a briefcase in his parents' wardrobe. Chappie thinks it must belong to his stepfather. Here's what happens:

❝I sat down and opened it. Inside are all these plastic bags, 30 or 40 of them filled with coins, mostly old quarters and Indian head nickels and even some weird-looking pennies with dates from way back in the early 1900s. Excellent discovery.

I took a couple of coins from each of about 6 bags so he wouldn't know any were missing if he happened to check, and put the bundle behind my mother's shoes in the closet where it had come from.

I had maybe 20 coins, small change, nothing bigger than a quarter and I took them to the pawnshop on Water Street near the old tannery where I knew some kids had hocked stuff. The old guy in there didn't say a word or even look at me when I spread the coins out on his counter and asked him how much he'd give me. He was this big fat guy with thick glasses and huge sweat circles under his arms and he scooped up the coins and took them in the back where he had an office. A few minutes later he comes out and says $80 which really blew my mind. Sounds fine to me, man, I told him and he paid me in twenties.

I went back to that coin collection in the closet a lot that summer, always taking only a few coins at a time from 6 or 7 different plastic bags. I was starting to figure out which ones were worth the most, like the dimes with the lady on it and the Indian head nickels and I'd just take those and mostly not bother with the others. Sometimes the guy at the pawnshop would give me fifty bucks, sometimes I'd get over a hundred.

Then one night I came home and I come up the steps carrying my bike and the door opens in front of me and it's my stepfather standing there with my mom right behind him with her face all red from crying.

pfp, 61 Gray's Inn Road, London WC1X 8TL May be photocopied for use within the purchasing institution only.
 ISBN 1 874050 39 2

He says, Get into the living room, Chappie, and sit down. We have some news for you, mister, he says, and that's when I remember the coins.

On the coffee table is the briefcase and when my stepfather flips it open I realize for the first time that there aren't very many of them left. It was kind of a shock. Some of the plastic bags were completely empty, although I didn't remember emptying any and leaving them in the briefcase, but it definitely looked like that's what I had done. Dumb. My mom sat down on the couch and looked at the open briefcase like it was a coffin with a body in it, and Ken said for me to sit in the chair which I did while he stood between me and the table and crossed his arms like some kind of a cop. I felt like a pathetic jerk sitting there looking at those few remaining coins.

Chappie, this is the worst thing you've ever done! my mom said and she started sobbing harder. She went sort of crazy then, screaming about how the coins had been her mother's and she'd given them to her years ago along with other precious and sentimental items and someday the coins were going to be mine and really valuable, but now I'd gone and stolen them and sold them so she'd never be able to pass them on to me. Never.

They were only coins, I said which was stupid but I didn't know what else to say and I was feeling really dumb anyhow and lowdown, so why not say something that sounded like I felt.

Sometimes that summer and during the fall too, I thought about going back and trying to make peace with my mom and my stepfather even, and offering to pay her back for the coins as soon as I got a job but I knew I could never pay her back because it wasn't the money. Those old coins of my grandmother's were like my inheritance.”

(Pause) Those coins in the story were old and quite rare, they were worth a lot more than their face value when they were first minted. But they had a value much higher than that – their sentimental value, their value to Chappie's family and that can't be measured in dollars or pounds.

The coins had been collected by Chappie's grandmother and were meant to be a gift from her to him long after her death, so that he could treasure them and see them increase in market value over many years and perhaps become rich through his grandmother's kindness. It's the circumstances and the people behind special things that give them a sentimental value which is much higher than face value or market value.

RESPONSE

Thankfulness and commitment

(Pause) Just think for a moment about what really matters in your life – what do you value most? You probably have something which is important to you – it means something special like the things *(Names of members of staff who spoke)* talked about at the start of our assembly. And those things get their value from how you live, what you believe – not from what they cost or how much you could sell them for. How would you feel if someone spoiled that thing or stole it?

If we lose sight of what really matters in our lives then we can end up making mistakes like Chappie. The choices you make depend on the values you have. In your day-to-day dealings with other people, in the choices you make, try and remember what really matters to you – and to them – then you'll be less likely to feel the regret that Chappie felt.

Extra Resources

The extract – much edited – is from Chapter 1 of Banks, R (1996) *Rule of the Bone*. London: Minerva. It is reproduced with kind permission.

Theme/ Key value

What's it worth?

Sense of personal responsibility

Title

Bin it and buy a new one?

Summary

This assembly uses a story to show that carelessness towards possessions can be destructive and wasteful and that a sense of personal responsibilty can have positive environmental effects.

Resources

Nothing at all.

REFLECTION

❝Lizzie sat cross-legged on her bed writing up the last page of her geography assignment. It wasn't easy, writing on the open ring-file spread across her knees. She looked over to her desk and wondered whether it was worth trying to clear a space to work. Her eyes assessed the enormity of the task. Books, files, hairdrier, drinks cans (some empty, some unopened), tapes and CDs (some in boxes, most just loose), bits of make-up, one earring – the one whose partner had been hoovered off the floor and mangled to death – and a carrier bag. She couldn't remember what was in the carrier bag. It had been there a long time.

Clearing a space big enough to write on would mean finding other places for things. What a hassle! Anyway, the chair was covered in discarded clothes, so Lizzie decided to stay put and do her homework on the bed.

She wanted to get it finished before Mum called her to go into town. They were going to find a top to go with the new jeans they'd bought last week. That had been hard work, persuading her mum to get her these jeans. Lizzie felt the label on the back pocket with some satisfaction, then she continued with her writing. Must get it finished. Then she wouldn't have to worry about it for the rest of the weekend. Just so long as she remembered to take it into school on Monday. Mr Longthorne had been adamant. 'Anyone turning up without a completed assignment on Monday will not be coming on the field trip with the rest of us,' he'd said. 'They'll stay in school and do extra written work.'

'No chance!' thought Lizzie. 'Not after I've got these new jeans specially!'

Well, her assigment was very nearly finished now. Lizzie murmured the words to herself as she wrote, 'caused by the last ice-age'. But the ink in her pen ran out on 'ice'. Lizzie swore, then looked about for a card of cartridges she knew she had somewhere. Window-sill perhaps? She craned her neck to peer behind the small dolls and the dirty coffee mugs. And what was that? The sun was bouncing like rainbow glitter off a compact disc. She stretched to pick up the disk just out of curiosity to see which one it was.

'So that's where it got to,' she said to herself as she read the label. But something was wrong. Close examination revealed the disc had a great scratch across it. Lizzie swore again. 'It'll never play now!' she said.

She spun the disc across the room to see if she could land it on the desk. It hit the edge and landed on the floor – right next to the card of cartridges. She leaned over to gather up the card and saw that there was in fact only one cartridge left, and that was badly squashed. 'Must have been trodden on,' thought Lizzie. 'Still, it's the only one I've got, so...'

She took the empty cartridge from her pen and slipped the new one into place. It jammed, so she pressed it hard with her thumb. And immediately a dark blue

pfp, 61 Gray's Inn Road, London WC1X 8TL ISBN 1 874050 39 2

fountain sprayed onto the duvet cover, while an inky trickle ran through her fingers and onto her jeans.

Lizzie's wail coincided with her mum's arrival at the door. 'You ready yet?' asked Mum. Then, 'What the...?'

As she came into the room she trod on the CD that Lizzie has thrown at the desk. And there followed one enormous row. Lizzie tried to point out that the cartridge must have had a crack in it. Mum didn't seem much bothered about the cartridge. She was too busy yelling about Lizzie's carelessness. The catalogue of complaints started with the jeans, of course. Lizzie was reminded they had cost her mother an arm and a leg. Then it was the duvet cover. Then it was all the tapes and CDs that were constantly being trodden on or left to gather dust. When Lizzie said she could always replace them that only made matters worse. How much money did she think they had that everything could be bought twice over – as well as all the new things she was always after? And not only that, but every time they went to the supermarket, wasn't Lizzie always the one going on about buying recycled everything? One, it was a waste of money buying things twice, and two wasn't it a waste of the world's resources buying tapes and CDs just to break them so that more have to produced! And okay, the earrings weren't solid gold but they had cost her gran a fair chunk of her pension for Lizzie's birthday.

The duvet cover was put to soak. But it seemed there would now be pale purple ink splashes forever across the pink squares and stripes. The jeans were more of a problem. The long dark stain at the top of the right leg wouldn't budge. And the scrubbing with the nail brush only left the fabric round the stain paler than before, with little tufts of white fluff.

'And before you even think it,' said her mother, 'you can't have new ones. It'll take me a month to recover from paying for these and they're only a week old!'

In the end, a compromise was reached. They would pay half each on the price of a pair of ordinary jeans form M&S. Lizzie wasn't happy – she had been adamant that it was Levi's she had to have. But she knew there was no way she'd get another pair. And, Mum said, on the way into town they'd call at the library with those overdue economics books, and Lizzie would pay the fine herself.

As Lizzie was about to ask, 'What overdue economics books?' her mother grabbed the carrier bag from the desk and Lizzie remembered.”

RESPONSE

Acknowledging failure and shortcomings

I expect we all know someone like Lizzie, careless with their possessions. *(Pause)* Perhaps you're like that sometimes. Did you notice what Lizzie's mum said about replacing spoiled things by buying new ones? Buying things twice is a waste of money and a waste of the Earth's resources. We live in a throw-away society and each of us needs to take some responsibility for that. In this school we try to do something about it *(mention any re-cycling/energy saving initiatives)* but we need to do something about it on a personal level too. *(Pause)*

We often think of 'waste' as empty hamburger boxes or the fries you leave because you've had enough. Being careless with personal possessions is a form of waste too.

In a moment of quiet, think about your own attitude to the things you own or buy. You could promise yourself to be less careless, less destructive. Or you could make that promise a prayer. *(Pause)*

Extra Resources

James, B (1991) *Recycling*. Hove: Wayland.
Knapp, B (1991) *Don't throw it away*. Reading: Atlantic Europe.

 ISBN 1 874050 39 2

Theme/ Key value

What's it worth?

Sense of personal responsibility

Title

The wrong trainers

Summary

This assembly uses a dialogue to help students reflect on the way in which material values, the media and peer group pressure can contrive to manipulate or influence our value judgements.

Resources

Two prepared students to read the dialogue. Reader 1 should be dressed in an old T-shirt and shorts and be barefoot. Reader 2 should wear normal school uniform or what he/she would usually wear to school.

REFLECTION

Reader 1: What are you doing after school?

Reader 2: Well, I'm going into town for some new trainers.

Reader 1: But you've only just bought some!

Reader 2: They're a week old, actually.

Reader 1: What – you've worn them out in a week? How many miles do you walk to school?

Reader 2: Don't be stupid! I just made a mistake. These were in the sale but they're last year's style. They look really naff now. The ones in the TV ads are in the shops now and they look the business. You must've seen them.

Reader 1: I never see TV. Anyway, is there a law in your country that says you can't wear last year's trainers once this year's are in the shops?

Reader 2: Of course not! But who wants to be seen in the wrong trainers?

Reader 1: So why didn't you wait 'till this week to buy new ones?

Reader 2: Because I didn't know the new range would be coming in, did I?

Reader 1: Oh – it's not on your calendar, then? 'New Trainers' Day?'

Reader 2: It's not a fixed date! It's just that every so often, the makers put out a new design and if you still have the old ones, then you're out-of-date aren't you?

Reader 1: I expect the makers introduce new ones when they reckon the old ones are worn out. They're obviously not very good quality, right?

Reader 2: Wrong! The best trainers would probably last for years. They're ergonomically designed and the materials are virtually indestructible even though they're extremely light. That's what the ads say, anyway. And loads of top athletes wear them.

Reader 1: But no-one actually knows how long they last because everyone gets new ones when the new range comes in.

Reader 2: That's right.

Reader 1: Well, I suppose you can buy new trainers so often because they're really cheap and you hardly notice the cost.

Reader 2: Are you kidding? The ones I bought last week cost an arm and a leg! And the new range will cost more than the old ones – they always do.

Reader 1: Why?

Reader 2: That's the way things are. Prices go up.

Reader 1: Who puts them up?

Reader 2: The makers, I suppose. I don't know – maybe the raw materials cost more.

Reader 1: Or maybe the makers know everyone will be buying the new style whatever the price, so they'll make even more money.

Reader 2: What do you mean, 'even more money'?

 ISBN 1 874050 39 2

Reader 1: Well, put yourself in their shoes – if you'll excuse the pun! If you make trainers that last for ten years, people only come back to buy new ones ten years later when the old ones wear out. You think to yourself, 'If only people would come back a bit sooner, I'd make a bit more money.' But you don't want to make trainers that wear out too quickly because your reputation could sink and you might lose business. Problem – how do you make good quality trainers that will last for years, but get people to come back for new ones before the old ones are worn out? Solution – persuade them they'll look a total freak in the old ones.

Reader 2: Oh – you should be on 'Mastermind'. Very clever stuff. Anyway, you're wrong. I've never yet seen a TV ad that says you look a freak in the old ones.

Reader 1: Not in so many words. But which ones do they show?

Reader 2: The new ones, of course! The ones they want you to buy!

Reader 1: And who do they show wearing them? People you wouldn't want to be seen in the street with? You know – teachers, parents and anoraks? No way! I bet they show big powerful athletes, or attractive, successful young people that you'd really like to be yourself.

Reader 2: Listen, for someone who never sees TV you seem to know an awful lot all of a sudden! For your information, the ads sometimes don't show people at all, so there!

Reader 1: Fair enough. But if you're watching an ad for the new range and you're wearing the old range, I bet whatever they show it doesn't make you think, 'Wow, my mates are going to be dead impressed when they see I'm still wearing last year's trainers. I'm so glad I haven't changed them'.

Reader 2: Oh, shut up will you! Anyway, I can't stay here all day. I've got to get into town.

Reader 1: What for?

Reader 2: I told you – I need some new trainers!

Reader 1: Need? Or just want?

Reader 2: All right then, I want some new trainers. *(Pause)* Can I have your old ones?

Reader 1: What for?

Reader 2: Where I come from, a pair of shoes costs half a year's wages. I had some old shoes once that the relief workers gave me. But they wore out ages ago. *(Pause)* I need some old trainers.

Reader 1: *(reflectively)* Need? Or just want?

Reader 2: What do you think?

RESPONSE

Thankfulness

It's easy to forget that shoes were invented to protect our feet and keep them warm! These days, many of the clothes we wear are fashion items that we buy because we know we'll feel good in them. And the latest styles have a special value. Our need for them is not really the need to be warm and covered – it's to fit in and look right. There's nothing wrong with this, but it's worth remembering that to be able to meet that kind of need is quite a luxurious position to be in. For some people in our community and for many people in other countries there is little or no choice. Their need for food and shelter and protection is the only thing that decides what they can have.

Action

We can choose to help others, even to feel some sense of responsibility for others and that can help make a better world. It is possible to understand that we are sometimes manipulated into spending money on things we want far more than things we need. And it's certainly possible to remember the difference between those things – what we want and what we need.

You make the choices – it's up to you. *(Pause)*

 ISBN 1 874050 39 2

Theme/ Key value

What's it worth?

Sense of personal responsibility

Title

Real riches

Summary This assembly uses the story of Jean Paul Getty to help the students consider what is of real value to them.

Resources Supplied OHT image (p72).

REFLECTION

■ ***Optional*** *Adapt the first two paragraphs if you haven't used this theme as a whole.*

Over the last few days we've been thinking about the value of things. We've seen the difference between basic material value, current market value and personal sentimental value. We've seen that some things have a hidden value because of what it costs in terms of the Earth's resources to make and replace them. And we've seen how some of us are rich enough to buy things simply because they suit the image we want, while others are too poor to buy things even though they provide the protection they need.

The other thing we've learned is that some things are worth more than money. But that's a hard lesson to learn and some people never learn it.

Jesus of Nazareth once said, 'Do not store up riches for yourself here on Earth, where moths and rust destroy, and robbers break in and steal. Instead, store up riches for yourselves in Heaven, where moths and rust cannot destroy, and robbers cannot break in and steal. For your heart will always be where your riches are.' *(Pause)* When Jesus used the words 'riches' he meant not only real objects but things like 'values' and 'love' – riches which cannot be costed.

Let me tell you a story about a fabulously wealthy man who, in spite of his money, seemed to find little happiness and whose family seemed to lack love and stability. As I read it, see if you can make the link between what Jesus said about riches and what happens in the story.

The man's name is Jean Paul Getty, and he died a little over twenty years ago aged eighty-four. Every night up until his death, he slept in his armchair with a shawl round his shoulders. He refused to go to bed to sleep because he thought if he lay down he would die – and he was afraid of dying.

He looked even older than his eighty-four years. During his life he'd had a series of face-lifts, but the last one had been a disastrous failure. The reason for the face-lifts was because for most of his life he had surrounded himself with beautiful women and he wanted them to find him attractive. And the reason for his lifestyle? He was the richest man in the world.

Getty was an American, who'd made a fortune out of oil. He'd also invested slices of his fortune in other businesses all over the world until he was making money so fast it became impossible to know how much he was worth.

Throughout his life he married three times, and had children. However, his passion, his hobby, and his only reason for living was making more and more money. Not spending it – just making it. Jean Paul Getty had no interest in family life and rarely saw his children. So it was perhaps not surprising that his children showed little interest in his business when they grew up. One became an academic. Another became addicted to drugs and was banished from the family. A third was banished simply because Getty couldn't stand his child's German grandfather.

 ISBN 1 874050 39 2

Everyone knew that Jean Paul Getty was the richest man in the world, so everyone imagined that the rest of the family also had access to untold wealth. But in fact, old Jean Paul kept his riches to himself, just using them to make more money. He thought of his children as a nuisance and not worthy of the Getty fortune.

The son who irritated him most was John Paul Junior, or John Paul the Second as he was known. He lived in London and spent years battling with his addiction to drink and drugs. When his marriage failed, his wife moved to Italy with their son, John Paul the Third, and their two daughters. This youngest John Paul was a painter, and while he was on a painting trip in Southern Italy he was kidnapped by a branch of the Mafia who were sure old Jean Paul would give Gail the money to pay a fat ransom. The boy was sixteen years old.

His parents each tried to phone the wealthy grandfather, but he refused to speak to them. During the four-month-long ordeal, his only comment was, 'I have fourteen grandchildren, and if I pay a penny of ransom, I'll have fourteen kidnapped children.' Let's not forget how rich he was. If necessary he could have paid 14 fat ransoms and never noticed.

Only when the kidnappers cut off young John Paul's ear and sent it in the post to a newspaper with a threat to kill their victim did his grandfather relent. But even then only slightly. He agreed to pay half the ransom and lend the boy's father the other half, to be paid back with interest.

A few days after the boy was released, it was the old man's birthday. Young John Paul tried to phone him to wish him happy birthday and thank him for paying the ransom. His grandfather refused to speak to him.

Do you think old Jean Paul was happy? Do you think his wealth seemed to have made him happy? As his life ebbed away, his greatest worry was what to do with his fortune. He didn't want to leave it to his family because he didn't feel that any of them deserved it – they had never shared his passion for money-making. And as his will revealed after his death, his faithful staff and the beautiful mistresses were not deemed to deserve anything either.

How happy would you be do you think, with all the money in the world, but no one to enjoy it with? America's richest man died alone and afraid, in his home in London, sitting in an armchair with a shawl round his shoulders. *(Pause)*

RESPONSE

- *Show supplied OHT image.*

Commitment

We have seen how people can have different forms of 'riches' – that the worth of something isn't always as simple as you might think. You've heard about the choices made by Jean Paul Getty and the consequences for him and those who knew him. I want you to think for a moment about the 'riches' you want. The choices you have to make. What's more important, the fast car or a healthy family? New clothes or happy friendships?

In this school we try and value a whole host of things which cost nothing in monetary terms. What do you value? As Jesus said, 'Your heart will always be where your riches are.' *(Pause)*

Extra Resources

The details about Jean Paul Getty are from Pearson, J (1995) *Painfully Rich: J. Paul Getty and his heirs.* London: Macmillan.

Theme

Discovery

Assemblies on this theme

1 The 'gift' of discovery
This assembly explores the nature of discovery and the qualities associated with it. It also seeks to show how these qualities have everyday applications which can relate to students' lives.

2 A moral dilemma – undiscovery?
This assembly looks at the debate concerning the discovery of nuclear fission and the building of nuclear weapons. The dilemma is what can be done, now that it has been discovered?

3 Run your race
This assembly aims to enable students to consider discovering their own potential by taking a positive attitude, working hard and using opportunities as they arise.

4 Out of this world?
This assembly looks at the importance of sharing discoveries, however big or small, so that others can learn from them.

5 A change for the better?
This assembly looks at the importance of discovering faith, as opposed to family and community influence. It uses Guru Nanak and the Dunblane tragedy as examples.

Record of use

Taken by	1	2	3	4	5
Date					
Given to					

Comments

 ISBN 1 874050 39 2

Discover **1.** To be the first to find or find out about. **2.** To learn about for the first time; realise. **3.** To reveal, to uncover; to make known.

Theme/ Key value

Discovery

Responding positively to questions about life

Title

The 'gift' of discovery

Summary

This assembly explores the nature of discovery and the qualities associated with it. It also seeks to show how these qualities have everyday applications which can relate to students' lives.

Resources

Supplied OHT image (p84). ***Optional*** A flip chart or OHT, with the following words: questioning, searching, looking beyond the immediate, open-mindedness, determination, courage, honesty, passion, concern for truth.

REFLECTION

An amazing thing about human beings is that throughout history there have been continual discoveries that have had an enormous impact on individuals, nations and cultures. For example, the invention of the wheel has had an unimaginable impact on travel and industry. Many things we take for granted today, like the electricity that powers microwave ovens, televisions and computers are discoveries that have drastically improved our standard of living.

■ ***Optional*** *Elaborate on examples which are appropriate to students' studies.*

But what does to 'discover' actually mean? Let's look at the dictionary definitions. They are from the Collins Dictionary.

■ *Show supplied OHT image.*

Here's the first one.

1 To be the first to find or find out about.

This is easy enough to understand, but it doesn't happen too often! 'To be the first to find or to find out about.' That's something like the discovery of the wheel, the harnessing of electrical power, or a mass of other things we take for granted. These sorts of discoveries have come from people who've often struggled for years to reach out into the unknown and who've found something that has had an enormous impact on all of us.

■ ***Optional*** *Ask the students what sorts of things fall into this category. Take examples, making sure they are 'firsts'.*

Maybe there's a future 'discoverer' in that sense here in our assembly – who knows? So what else does the dictionary say?

2 To learn about for the first time; realise

We can all identify with that. This is the unique wonder which is within us all – as long as we're open-minded none of us will ever stop discovering new things. It doesn't matter how old we are either. I can continue to find things which are new to me just as you can – although it's also part of my job as a teacher to try to help you discover things. It's part of the reason you come to school.

So, what are examples of this? How about the young child learning how to swim. People have always known how to swim – swimming itself is not a new discovery. But for that young child suddenly doing it for the first time, it really is a discovery. That moment when you push off from the side of the pool, without help, and suddenly you're splashing about and not sinking!

■ ***Optional*** *Use an example of your own here instead of the following story – perhaps a new skill you learnt as an adult. If you do so, still use the final sentences of the paragraph: 'There I was...today.'*

I remember being about eight years old and sitting on a bike which was a little big for me, with my cousin Ann holding on to the back of the saddle to steady me. We moved off and for a few wobbly moments I turned the pedals and said something to Ann in a breathless voice, but she didn't

 ISBN 1 874050 39 2

answer because she'd let go! There I was, discovering something millions of other people all over the world could do. But for me it was a moment of pure joy and exhilaration. 'To learn for the first time.' Perhaps that will happen to you today.

Now the final dictionary definition.

3 To reveal, to uncover; to make known.

This is a bit harder to get to grips with. It has to do with trying to make sense of how we live together, to find out reasons for things. It's perhaps the hardest kind of discovery – one person will believe that they have discoverd the truth about why we do something, but another will disagree – and who's to say which person is right? But often these beliefs do share insights which can help us to discover things about ourselves. For example, the truth revealed by the Christian Bible which says that people can't live by bread alone. This makes us think. It's trying to give us a different type of discovery – a moral discovery.

■ ***Optional*** *Ask the students what they think the phrase 'people cannot live…' means.*

The great thinkers and philosophers have often spent their whole adult lives grappling with spiritual, moral and philosophical ideas to try to reveal how we can live with purpose and in harmony. Many of these people became religious leaders and their 'discoveries' have had an impact on millions of people's lives – perhaps including your own.

So, scientists, explorers, thinkers, engineers, artists and many other groups have made discoveries down the ages. These discoverers had an extraordinary desire to discover things about – and to understand – the world we live in, and to improve the life we live. But it's important to remember that their great discoveries, even those which happened by chance or in a flash of inspiration, were preceded by another type of reaching into the unknown – their self-discovery.

It's a well-known saying amongst scientists that for every one successful discovery there are at least one hundred failures. It's during these times of failure that many people discover important things about themselves – not just their intelligence and creativity, but also their belief in their convictions and skills, their ability and strength to learn and persist, and their resolve to succeed.

Let's just take a moment to think about what else they might discover about themselves. What do you think these qualities might be?

■ ***Optional*** *Use the flip chart or OHT. Take some answers from the students and compare them with those written on it.*

Here are some: questioning, searching, looking beyond the immediate, open-mindedness, determination, courage, honesty, passion, concern for truth.

RESPONSE

Thankfulness

We all have the opportunity to discover things every day. Not things which are going to revolutionise the world like the wheel – although perhaps one day one of you will discover something like that. But we have opportunities to discover new things for ourselves and about ourselves. And that's a great opportunity to have, and one we can be thankful for and take every opportunity to exploit. It's often all too easy to shut ourselves down and stop learning and finding new things. But finding new things helps us to grow, develop, change and remain active and interesting people.

If you believe in a God, you might like to take a moment to say thank you for the gift of discovery you have been given.

Commitment

Explorers and scientists aren't the only people who make discoveries. Discovery is part of everyone's life. *(Pause)* Think of those qualities we talked about earlier – and resolve to apply them to whatever you do. The way you do things in school, the way you act with friends and family. Remember this amazing 'gift' of discovery is not just for somebody else. It's for you.

Theme/ Key value

Discovery

Responding positively to questions about life

Title

A moral dilemma – undiscovery?

Summary

This assembly looks at the debate concerning the discovery of nuclear fission and the building of nuclear weapons. The dilemma is what can be done, now that it has been discovered?

Resources

Three students (good readers)/teachers for this debate (they could be dressed according to their characters). It would be possible for the person taking the assembly to read the parts instead.

REFLECTION

Welcome to the chat show called 'Moral Dilemma', the show that looks at issues to which there appear to be no right answers. Today we are discussing what is perhaps one of the most difficult issues of all – nuclear fission and the building of nuclear weapons.

We have three special guests. Professor Jennifer Cartwright, who has wide experience in scientific research.

- *Applause and encourage the students to join in.*

Takae Ishii, a survivor from Hiroshima.

- *Applause.*

And Sir Antony Dury, Member of Parliament. Welcome to our panel!

The discovery of nuclear fission and the building of nuclear weapons has prompted perhaps the greatest debate this century. It is not only due to the fact that just six years after the discovery of nuclear fission it's energy was used to destroy the cities of Hiroshima and Nagasaki. But it is also the extent of the devastation and the continuing effects of it which continue to provoke serious questions.

Let's begin with a reminder of the facts. Professor Cartwright, can you explain to us in simple terms what nuclear fission is?

Reader 1: Certainly. Put simply, scientists working in the 1930s and 40s discovered that by splitting the atom they could causes an energy-releasing chain reaction which could produce vast amounts of power. This process is what is known as nuclear fission and since its discovery the power has brought great benefits to humanity. But, of course, that sort of power is not only useful for peaceful purposes. It can also be used for destructive purposes, and it was only shortly after its discovery that Franklin D. Roosevelt, the US President at the time, was alerted to this fact. In response he created a team to design and build the world's first atomic bomb.

And its first use as a weapon was the bomb which was dropped on Hiroshima on the 6th of August 1945, followed by another, three days later, on Nagasaki. This was only very shortly after the first discovery of nuclear fission, and has since raised many questions about how much was actually known about its effects. Approximately two hundred thousand people were killed by the two bombs, and thousands more died later from the effects of radiation. Sir Antony, do you believe that was the right thing to do?

Reader 2: This question has haunted the American government ever since. *(Pause)* The decision was made because it was felt that the war against Japan could drag on, and already both American and British forces had lost many lives. The intention was to frighten the Japanese into an immediate surrender, and in this it succeeded. So viewed in this light, it could be argued that the decision was justified. Possibly the British prisoners-of-war held by the Japanese were glad it was dropped, because it probably saved their lives. But when you think about the horrific civilian loss of life and suffering – and the suffering of both Japanese and American people ever since

 ISBN 1 874050 39 2

which would appear to be the result of radiation – it makes you wonder what was right and what was wrong.

Takae, you were in Hiroshima at the time of the bombing and miraculously survived. What do you remember?

Reader 3: I remember the day as if it happened only yesterday. An alarm was sounded and we feared it was a heavy American attack so we hurriedly returned home. We heaved a sigh of relief when the alarm was finally called off. Suddenly, on that splendid Summer day, there was a tremendous flash and a moment later the whole sky burst into flames. It was like being in the middle of a huge firework display. My mother threw herself on top of me and in that instant the house collapsed on us with a resounding crash. I don't know what happened afterwards. It was as if time stopped. Gradually we began to make out sounds coming from outside. We could hear weeping and shouting. Eventually, we made our way through fallen beams and rubble out into the open. Not a single house was still standing and the trees, which just a short time before had been a mass of green foliage, were reduced to ash... We thought it was dangerous to stay where we were and we decided to go to a large garden that belonged to the old nobility of Hiroshima, but when we got there, it was unrecognisable. The next morning we returned home. The city was a pile of rubble, and naked bodies burnt to cinders littered the streets. The horror of war did not come to an end with the declaration of peace. First of all there was the mammoth task of burning all the bodies. Then there were the effects of radiation.

Listening to Takae's testimony, Professor, do you think that the Americans were justified in dropping the two bombs?

Reader 1: It was a difficult decision and, of course, the loss of life and subsequent deaths and illnesses were horrific. But think about this: since we've had nuclear weapons, the world has not seen a major conflict on anything like the scale of the two world wars. Nuclear weapons have kept the peace – admittedly through fear, but the risk of global destruction is not one any country is prepared to undertake. So in the long run, for the sake of all humanity, I think the demonstration of the bomb's awesome power was justified.

Thank you, Professor. How about you, Sir Antony? What are your thoughts?

Reader 2: Well, it's true we've not had a major world war since 1945, but we've come pretty close. With more and more countries now making their own nuclear weapons, who knows how long it will be before some madman is prepared to use them? If we could destroy all the nuclear arsenals I would sleep sounder at night, but once the scientists have discovered something it's impossible to 'undiscover' it!

RESPONSE

What do you think? *(Pause)* That's the real problem isn't it? Once we know something, we can't unknow it. Once we discover something, we can't undiscover it. Can this dilemma ever be solved? Albert Einstein once wrote, 'On the assumption that a Third World War must escalate to nuclear destruction, I can tell you that the Fourth World War will be fought with bows and arrows.' *(Pause)*

Commitment

Let us spend a quiet moment thinking about the importance of using all discoveries, whatever they are, to benefit and not hinder the progress we make as a nation as a community and as individuals. And if you believe in a God, pray that this would be the case, and that governments throughout the world, especially the major world powers, will always act with wisdom and responsibility.

Extra Resources

Challener, J (1995) *The Visual Dictionary of Physics.* London: Dorling Kindersley. Maruki, T (1980) *The Hiroshima Story.* London: A & C Black. Yass, M (1971) *Hiroshima.* Hove: Wayland.

Note: The name Antony Dury is fictitious.

Theme/ Key value

Discovery

Responding positively to questions about life

Title

Run your race

Summary

This assembly aims to enable students to consider discovering their own potential by taking a positive attitude, working hard and using opportunities as they arise.

Resources

Optional Two students to read the short dialogue.

REFLECTION

Optional *Two students on stage. Student 1 is dressed as an athlete, student 2 in school uniform. Student 1 is stretching, doing press-ups, etc., and student 2 is lazing about.*

Student 1: Are you coming to training today?

Student 2: No. I can't be bothered.

Student 1: What? *(Name of a sports teacher)* is going to choose the team to run in the finals.

Student 2: Yeah, but I'm just not good enough, and I don't know why you're going either because what hope have you got? I mean, even I beat you last year!

Student 1: You're good enough, you just don't train. Anyway, I'm going to give it a go and see what happens. See you around!

How often do you hear the phrase: 'I can't do it!' or 'I'm not good enough!'? How often have you said it yourself? *(Pause)* More often than not, when you look at it a little closer, the person is actually saying, 'I can't be bothered!' or 'I'm not prepared to make the effort in case I look a fool!' Such an approach to life results in missing out not only on the possibility of achieving something, but more importantly, discovering something more about yourself and what you can do!

All of us here, I imagine, want to succeed at something. Whether it's in school, a job, a particular sport, or even just getting on well with other people – we all basically want to do well. The problem is that sometimes we don't really know what we're good at. Family, friends and school can often push you in certain directions – tell you what's good for you. But maybe you don't want to go that way. Maybe you want to try something else.

So think for a moment. What can I do? What am I capable of? Do I actually know? *(Pause)* When you consider great people in history who have been able to realise their potential and even become legends in their own field, one common feature is that they have worked hard to make their lives a success.

They were people who were committed to discovering and nurturing their potential, whatever the pressure and sometimes conflict, and were dedicated to doing something about it. Charles Darwin and Marie Curie, for example, are two people who had to struggle. But they both had self-belief and were committed to their interests. Through dedication and hard work, they were able to make discoveries that affect us all, even today.

Another common feature in such people is that in discovering their vocation in life, they make the most of the opportunities which arise. A striking example is the story of a black American girl called Wilma Rudolf who was paralysed from birth. However, when she was eight, she was told that a cure had been found, and that she would soon be walking. After she had received the treatment that cured her, her doctor told her, 'It's up to you now, you're healed! You'll be able to walk but it won't be easy – you're going to have to fight!' But Wilma was so grateful for this opportunity to walk and do all the things that she had missed out on as a young girl, that not

 ISBN 1 874050 39 2

only did she fight to walk properly, but she also struggled to run as well. In doing so, she discovered that she actually had great potential as an athlete. So much so, that a few years later in the 1960 Olympic Games, she became the fastest woman in the world, winning the 100m, 200m and 4x100m sprint medals.

The history of the Olympic Games is full of remarkable stories. In the 1906 Olympics, there was a middle distance runner called George Bonhag. He trained extremely hard and was expected to win his event. But for reasons he couldn't explain, he failed. He came last. He was so distraught that people thought he would pack his bags and slip away. But he didn't. He went back to the organisers and said, 'Look, I've failed, I'm embarrassed and ashamed that I've let everyone down. Is there any other event that I can have a go at? I want to have another go.' Well this was a time when Olympic organisers were more casual about such things, and they said, 'Well, actually, someone has dropped out of an event only this morning'. George said, 'Put me in!' As he was going out of the door, he said, 'Oh, by the way, what is it?' They said it was the mile walk. And off he went to practise walking round the track.

There were no heats, just the final. George lined up with the other competitors and suddenly they were off round the track. After one lap he was half a lap down. After two they had lapped him, and after three, he was another half a lap down. And the interest was would he be lapped a second time, because that would be a world record.

All the group were pretty evenly matched as they came round the final bend with George Bonhag in their sights. And then something extraordinary happened; the front athlete was so keen to win he increased his speed to the point where he was actually breaking the rules – technically he was running. Then the walker in second place did the same thing, and then the next one, and suddenly the whole group was running for the line, except George. After his disappointment in his own race he was determined to win a medal. Rather than follow the others, he carried on walking. All the athletes were disqualified – except for George. If you look in the record books, George Bonhag won a gold medal.

Two very different and yet remarkable stories about people who simply made the most of the opportunities that arose. They were prepared to run the race, and they gave it their best shot! Like Wilma and George, sometimes we need determination and persistence to discover the truth about ourselves.

RESPONSE

Action

My 'race' is different from yours. I can't run your race and you can't run mine! In fact we all have individual races to run in life, so comparing ourselves to others isn't very helpful. What we all need to do is to discover what we are able to do, and to simply set about doing our best.

Commitment

Let each one of us reflect on the things in our lives which we are good at or things that with some effort we could be good at. Perhaps you are the sort of person who is good at putting other people at their ease. Perhaps you have lots of confidence. Perhaps you are good at sport. Perhaps you are a good team player.

As we think about how self-discovery or self-realisation take determination and persistence, you may wish to make a commitment to yourself. To redouble your efforts and develop your talents to the best of your ability, to realise your potential. Those of you who believe in a God, may also wish to offer your skills and talents to his service.

Extra Resources

Greenberg, S (1996) *The Olympic Book of Facts and Feats.* Enfield: Guinness.

 ISBN 1 874050 39 2

Theme/ Key value

Discovery

Responding positively to questions about life

Title

Out of this world?

Summary

This assembly looks at the importance of sharing discoveries, however big or small, so that others can learn from them.

Resources

A good reader to read the Armstrong extract. ***Optional*** A few students to share an experience (which has been written down in preparation). Supplied OHT image (p84).

REFLECTION

■ *Show supplied OHT image throughout the assembly.*

What does the phrase 'out of this world' mean to you? Some people use it when referring to something they have seen, like watching a really good film. Other people use it to describe a fantastic experience they have had, that often includes both fear and excitement, such as going on a big roller-coaster ride or experiencing a dramatic simulator in a theme park.

■ ***Optional*** *Introduce the students who will describe what 'out of this world' means to them. The students then read out their short prepared pieces. Thank them and dismiss them.*

Very few people have been able to use the phrase 'out of this world' in the literal sense, but Neil Armstrong is one of them. On the 20th of July 1969, he stepped off the lunar landing vehicle 'Eagle' at 03.56 British Summer Time and planted his left foot on the moon's surface, proclaiming, 'That's one small step for man, one giant leap for mankind'. Neil Armstrong, Commander of Apollo 11, was the first man ever to walk on the moon. For him, it certainly was 'out of this world!'

But for most of us it means something to do with discovery. It can be simple things or complex things. For example, I remember the first time I tasted *(describe a memorable taste experience or similar here).* A girl I know finished a series of hard exams and promised herself she'd celebrate by trying two things which were completely out of character: surfing and parachuting. The waiting around and the relative short thrill that went with parachuting did very little for her but the surfing she loved. The feeling it gave her she would describe as 'out of this world', and it really was a discovery for her. She had lessons, persuaded a group of friends to join her, and now they meet up in Cornwall whenever they can.

That's one of the things about any 'discovery' – it needs to be shared, whatever it is, however great or small.

How many of you, having had an amazing experience, want to keep it to yourselves?

■ ***Optional*** *Choose a relevant example.*

Most of us, I imagine, want to tell our friends straightaway and let them share and enjoy the experience. And this has always happened. Whatever the consequences, discoveries throughout history have been shared and recognised by others. It's only by doing that that we can learn from what's been discovered – whether it's an idea, an experience or a wonderful taste!

Neil Armstrong, whom I mentioned earlier, made one of the most amazing 'out of this world' discoveries by going to the moon. Just listen for a moment to what he said and share in his experience.

❝The most dramatic recollections I had were the sights themselves. Of all the spectacular views we had, the most impressive to me was on the way to the moon, when we flew through its shadow. We were still thousands of miles away, but close enough, so that the moon almost filled our circular window. It was eclipsing the sun, from our position, and the corona of the sun was visible around the limb of the moon as a gigantic lens-shaped or saucer-shaped light, stretching out to several lunar diameters. It was magnificent, but the moon was even more so. We were in its shadow, so there was no part of it illuminated by the sun. It was illuminated only by earthshine. It made the moon appear blue-grey, and the entire scene looked decidedly three-dimensional... I was sure that it would be an hospitable host. It had been awaiting its first visitors for a long time. After touch down I reported back to Earth. The sky is black, you know. It's a very dark sky. But it seemed more like daylight than darkness as we looked out the window. It's a peculiar thing, but the surface looked very warm and inviting. It was the sort of situation in which you felt like going out there in nothing but a swimming suit to get a little sun. From the cockpit, the surface seemed to be tan. It's hard to account for that, because later when I held this material in my hand, it wasn't tan at all. It was black, grey and so on. It's some kind of lighting effect, but out the window the surface looks much more like desert sand than black sand...”

An amazing discovery, so much so that after their return to Earth, Aldrin, Armstrong, and the command pilot Michael Collins made a round-the-world goodwill tour to talk about the trip.

Thankfulness

RESPONSE

Although the Apollo astronauts discovered many important scientific facts, they also discovered something else – something that for some of them at least was more important than moon dust. It seems that by being out in space and looking back at the entire world floating there in the darkness of eternity they experienced a spiritual discovery. Over the years they've shared this sense of wonder and awe with thousands of their fellow human beings. They discovered the belief that there is something greater than life on Earth .

Commitment

Clearly, very few people become pioneers like Neil Armstrong and discover something new for humanity for the first time. But we can all have 'out of this world' experiences as we explore the world around us and venture into new territory. Whatever the situation, let us learn to share our discoveries, and similarly be willing to enjoy those of others around us, whatever they may be!

If you believe in a God you might like to pray for a few moments that you will continue to make new discoveries and be able to share them with others. If you don't have such a belief you could just reflect on the amazing wonders of our world and decide to make your own discoveries as well as learn from others.

Extra Resources

There is an appropriate poem to go with this assembly in Simon, S (ed) (1995) *Star Walk*. New York: Morrow Junior Books. Relevant information is available in Furniss, T (1989) *One Small Step The Apollo Missions: a 20 Year Perspective*. Yeovil: Haynes and Docherty, P (ed) (1993) *The Visual Dictionary Of the Universe*. London: Dorling Kindersley.

Theme/ Key value

Discovery

Responding positively to questions about life

Title

A change for the better?

Summary

This assembly looks at the importance of discovering faith, as opposed to family and community influence. It uses Guru Nanak and the Dunblane tragedy as examples.

Resources

Optional Student to read the extract at the end.

REFLECTION

What is the biggest change that has ever happened in your life? *(Pause)* As you consider the question, no doubt things like moving house, changing schools and making new friends come to mind. But for many people the biggest change actually has nothing to do with material things at all. In fact it is to do with a change in what they were brought up to believe and a search to discover a better way of living.

One man who made an important personal discovery of faith was Guru Nanak, the founder of Sikhism. There are thousands of Sikhs living in Britain today who know many of the wonderful stories about him.

- ***Optional*** *If you have a Sikh community in your area or Sikh students you can refer to these at this point.*

Guru Nanak was born in 1469 in the village of Talwandi, which is now in Pakistan. At the time, it was an area that was deeply divided between Muslims and Hindus. Nanak's family and most of his village were Hindu, but he had Muslim neighbours and he did not allow the religious differences he saw make any difference to the way he treated people. For example, when he was still a boy, his father gave him twenty rupees, and sent him to the nearby town saying: 'Do the best business you can'. However, on his way, he came across twenty holy men, who looked extremely hungry. When he discovered that they had not eaten for a week, he hurried to the town and bought baskets of food with the money his father had given him, and carried them back to the holy men. When his father discovered what he had done with the money, he was both angry and yet dumbfounded. His son had wasted all the money and yet had explained that he had done the best business he could think of – he had helped to feed the hungry.
From an early age, Nanak showed unusual devotion to God. He spent many hours in prayer and meditation, and could often be heard singing hymns he had written, giving praise to God. Even while he was working as a clerk for a local landowner (who was Muslim), his mind often turned to thoughts about God. One day, when he went to the river to bathe at dawn – which was a normal custom for Hindus then as it still is today – he failed to return. After a while his friends told his employer, who ordered a search and the villagers dragged the river. Nanak could not be found. Then, three days later, he reappeared at his home. He did not speak for a day – which his family must have found extremely difficult to understand, especially as they thought he must have drowned. But when he did speak it became clear that he had made a great discovery. He said, 'There is neither Hindu nor Muslim, only brothers and sisters – so whose path shall I follow? I shall follow God's path. God is neither Hindu nor Muslim and the path I follow is God's'.

This was the turning point in his life – the biggest change. He was not criticising either faith, but he was saying that any path was right if it led to God. It was wrong if it did not. God was in the heart, not in a mosque or temple, or in religious

 ISBN 1 874050 39 2

ceremonies and formal prayers. It did not matter what faith you were so long as you genuinely sought after God, whom he described as, 'One…the truth… Creator… without hate'. This is a message shared by the Christian faith too.

For the next twenty years Nanak travelled thousands of miles, teaching about God and how God wants us to act towards other people. For example, he insisted that everyone was equal, so that whether you were rich or poor, woman or man, prince or beggar, you should all be able to sit at the same table and share a meal together. This was something unheard of in India at the time and is still a challenging idea today.

When he was fifty, Nanak founded a town in the Punjab called Kartarpur. Here many people came to visit him and learn from his wisdom, and become his sikhs or disciples who in turn continued the faith that Nanak had begun.

RESPONSE

Thankfulness and celebration

Like Nanak, we are all brought up to have certain beliefs, and these stem from our parents and home surroundings. Some of these beliefs are concerned with whether there is a God or not, and the nature of God. But many are to do with people around us, and how we view them. Let's be thankful and celebrate the fact that there is a rich variety of beliefs in our society, and many of us here will have very different beliefs, especially when it comes to God. But it is easy to take them for granted, and not think about what we actually believe, why we behave in the way we do towards other people, and whether we need to change. In short, there is a need to ask the question that Nanak, and many people before and after him have asked: Have I made my own discovery of faith? What do I actually believe?

Action

One final thought. It concerns the tragic Dunblane massacre of sixteen children and their teacher, which affected not only a small Scottish community, but also the whole nation. In the aftermath of the killings, many people came to the school to grieve. Reverend John Drane was one of the many clergymen, trying to help the people in their suffering. One night, he saw a gang of youths, aged seventeen to twenty, gather outside the school and light sixteen candles. They asked him to say something suitable, but with tears streaming down his face, he could only say a short prayer. Then he witnessed an amazing change. This is what he wrote:

■ ***Optional*** *Ask the student to read this passage.*

"A question came first: 'What kind of world is this?' Another asked: 'Is there any hope?' Someone said: 'I wish I could trust God.' 'I'll need to change,' said a fourth one. As he did so, he looked first at me and then glanced over his shoulder to the police who were on duty. He reached into his pocket and I could see he had a knife. He knelt again by the ring of candles and quietly said: 'I'll not be needing this now,' as he tucked it away under some of the flowers lying nearby. One of the others produced what looked like a piece of cycle chain, and did the same. We stood silently for a moment, and then we went our separate ways.

Was God in Dunblane? Of course. How could I have been so foolish as to doubt it? This was holy ground, and those youths were meeting God in a profound way. Though they would not have expressed it in this way, they were repenting (which means turning round). They were reaching out. They were searching for a better way of living."

■ ***Optional*** *If a student has read, thank him or her.*

Extra Resources

Penney, S (1988) *Sikhism*. Oxford: Heinemann. Essex County Council Education (1995) *Teaching about World Faiths: curriculum support for teachers*. Breuilly, E and Palmer, S. (1993) *Sainsbury's Religions of the World*. London: HarperCollins.

 ISBN 1 874050 39 2

Theme

Journeys

Assemblies on this theme

1 **Life's like that**
This assembly aims to get students to reflect on their own choices and decisions by using the metaphor of life as a journey.

2 **Personal journeys**
This assembly uses the real-life examples of two people connected with the school community to demonstrate the qualities needed to take advantage of unexpected turning points in life. It encourages students to reflect on similar qualities they might have to help them make the most of what lies ahead.

3 **From country to country**
This assembly asks students to consider changes of direction in their lives in comparison with the plight of refugees and asylum seekers. It aims to help students gain a sense of perspective when making important decisions.

4 **Rites of passage**
This assembly shows how the major religions' rites of passage and pilgrimage sites stand as patterns for those who want their life journeys to include a spiritual quest.

5 **The excitement of journeying**
This assembly uses real examples of concern being shown for young people who were at a turning point in their lives and suggests that we have some control over the directions we take.

Record of use

	1	2	3	4	5
Taken by					
Date					
Given to					

Comments

pfp, 61 Gray's Inn Road, London WC1X 8TL ISBN 1 874050 39 2

JOURNEYS • OHT

 ISBN 1 874050 39 2

Theme/ Key value

Journeys

Valuing progress and achievement

Title

Life's like that

Summary

This assembly aims to get students to reflect on their own choices and decisions by using the metaphor of life as a journey.

Resources

Supplied OHT image (p96).

REFLECTION

"Gemma had spent a few days in London with her grandparents and now they were driving her back to Leeds, where she lived with her mum. It looked like a straightforward journey. She and her grandad had checked it in the road map book before they left. Straight up the M1, no problem.

Progress between London and Milton Keynes was pretty fast and uneventful. Gemma watched out for the signposts. Soon after Milton Keynes she saw 'Northampton 10'. She'd already worked out that when they reached Northampton they'd have done one third of their journey. Just past Northampton they saw a sign for a service area, and they pulled off for a trip to the loo and a snack.

Gemma fancied a walk round the shop too, so after they'd all had a coffee, that's where they went. Grandad bought her a couple of tapes to play on the car cassette player, before they were hurried out by Gran who pointed out that they'd been there for over half an hour.

Eventually they got back on the road, but this time progress was very slow – partly because of roadworks and partly because of the weight of traffic. In fact, just past the turning point for Derby everything came to a standstill for a full ten minutes. Not much in a journey of four hours, but it seemed like an age while they all sat there doing nothing.

Well, that's not strictly true, because Gemma complained a lot. Grandad tried to explain how heavy traffic ahead could bunch up and cause the following traffic to slow down and even stop for a while. But Gemma wasn't interested. She just wanted to get going.

When they were on the move again, Gemma watched for the signs. They planned to have lunch after Wakefield, but she knew that the turnings to Nottingham and Sheffield came before that. Before they got to Sheffield, there was another turning to a service area. Gemma said she needed the loo. It was only half true. She knew they didn't really have the time, but she was really hoping to find something she'd seen at the first service area. Yes – there it was near the other games machines. It was a ski slalom simulator and it looked really good. So once again Grandad came up with the money and Gemma skied her way down the electronic ski-run pictured on the big screen.

Further hold-ups for road works meant they had a very late lunch. It was also a very fast one. Grandad insisted that because they'd lost so much time they'd have to buy sandwiches and eat them in the car as he drove. Even so, they were an hour later than they'd hoped when they finally reached Gemma's house. Her mum said she expected the roadworks were to blame. Or the heavy traffic. But Gran said it was their own fault, too. They'd chosen to take the extra turn-off without realising how much time it would cost them."

■ *Show supplied OHT image.*

Okay – perhaps that wasn't a truly riveting story, but I bet it was pretty familiar to some people here. The reason I told it is that it's a useful way of helping us to think of a different kind of journey – a journey we all have to make. I'm talking about the journey through life. For most of you, the first part of your journey through life probably started off fairly easily, with few worries or decisions for you to make. When you needed anything, or sometimes

pfp, 61 Gray's Inn Road, London WC1X 8TL ISBN 1 874050 39 2

even just fancied having something, someone was there to make sure you got it – like Grandad at the service area shop. Later on, you started to learn a few things. That there are sometimes signs that point you in the right direction for where you want to go, for example, or that offer you the choice of some interesting diversions. And you learn that the choices you make have consequences. That's a bit like Gemma choosing to stop and play on the ski simulator. She didn't think about it at the time, but soon had to realise that her decision had helped to make them all late.

Of course, sometimes life doesn't go the way you want it to, and it's not really your fault, but you still can't do much about it. That's like being stuck because of roadworks. When things don't go the way you want, do you try to understand and be patient? Or do you do what Gemma did, and complain and get cross? *(Pause)*

Some time after that journey with her grandparents, Gemma had to make some important choices. When she was sixteen she'd reached one of life's milestones, the one where she had to decide whether to stay on at school and do A-levels, or go to the local college and get some GNVQs. There were no guarantees of a job whichever route she took. It was a case of trying to think ahead – of thinking about what sort of journey she'd like her life to be. There are a good few decisions like this that we have to make throughout our lives – important decisions.

But some people give the same amount of thought to important choices like that as they do to choosing whether or not to go on a ski machine. Those people haven't realised that the turning points, milestones, choices and destinations along life's journey are opportunities that give us chances: chances to think; to look back at the choices we made in the past; to look forward to the destinations we hope to reach in the future; to assess what the best route is for reaching them.

That all sounds a bit heavy doesn't it? But remember another thing, too. By giving careful thought to those decisions, you're also doing something else. You're giving yourself the best chance to experience all the adventures, surprises, opportunities and sheer excitement that a journey can give you. *(Pause)*

RESPONSE

Here's a short poem about travelling into the future. It uses the image of climbing a mountain, and gives a stirring taste of the excitement there is for all of us as we progress on our journeys through life.

> I am being driven forward
> Into an unknown land
> The pass grows steeper
> The air colder and sharper
> A wind from my unknown goal
> Stirs the strings
> Of expectation.

Commitment and action

When you're thinking seriously about making an important choice at one of life's milestones or turning points, here are three questions you could ask yourself: What's my goal? Have I chosen it carefully? How much do I want to achieve it? If you have a faith, you may believe that your god is guiding you. There is a verse in the Jewish and Christian scriptures about this. It says: 'If you wander off the road to the right or the left, you will hear his voice behind you saying, "Here is the road. Follow it".'

We only experience the excitement of the mountain tops if we make an effort. Are you determined to make an effort? If you're clear about your goal, perhaps you might like to make a commitment to yourself to go for it, and not get diverted into the 'amusement arcades' of life!

Extra Resources

The Bible reference is from the *Good News Bible*, Isaiah Chapter 30, verse 21.
The poem is by Dag Hammarskjöld, published in *Markings* (London: Faber and Faber, 1964) and reproduced with kind permission.

Theme/ Key value

Journeys

Valuing progress and achievement

Title

Personal journeys

Summary

This assembly uses the real-life examples of two people connected with the school community to demonstrate the qualities needed to take advantage of unexpected turning points in one's life. It encourages students to reflect on similar qualities they might have or could develop which would help them make the most of whatever lies ahead.

Resources

Two people to be interviewed about their life journey (see below). Your two volunteers should be people who have taken a chosen or unplanned new direction at some stage in their lives. The ideal would be a teacher or other person working in school who once did a different job, and a former student of your school who is not following the career they first went for. The student should be typical of your school, eg. not the exception who went to Oxbridge or a young offender institution. Let them know the questions beforehand.

REFLECTION

- *Introduce the two guests.*
- *Interview them one at a time. Encourage them to tell their story by asking questions that contain the theme's key words – turning points, milestones, choices, destinations and the qualities they showed in making their decisions.*
- *Here are some sample questions you might use for the school employee:*

1 Tell us a bit about yourself. For example, where did you go to school?

2 Leaving school is a major milestone in anyone's life. What did you do when you left school?

3 What made you choose this direction?

4 Why did you have that particular destination in view?

5 You obviously came to a major turning point when you decided to change jobs and become a teacher *(or whatever)*. What made you change your mind?

6 Did this cause any difficulties for you?

7 If someone had told you at the time you were leaving school that one day you'd be a teacher *(or whatever)*, what would your reaction have been?

8 Are you surprised that your life journey has taken a different route to what you first planned? Are you glad you chose to take the turning to a new destination?

- *Here are some sample questions you might use for the former student:*

1 Tell us a bit about yourself. When were you at this school?

2 And what are you doing now?

3 What were your best subjects at school?

4 What did you want to do when you left school? What was your planned 'destination'?

5 How did you plan to reach that destination?

6 What governed your choices at that time?

7 What happened to those plans?

8 At what point did you realise you would have to take a new direction?

9 If someone had told you when you were leaving school that one day you'd be doing *(whatever)*, what would your reaction have been?

 ISBN 1 874050 39 2

10 What advice would you give to someone who is faced with having to change their plans?

■ *At the end of the interviews, thank both volunteers then continue.*

Let's think for a moment about the personal qualities each of these people have which helped them to choose their directions in life, and have given them the ability to continue on their chosen paths.

RESPONSE

■ *Mention any outstanding features that emerged from what your volunteers said. For example, their strength, determination, good humour, self assurance, perseverance.*

Action

Nobody knows where their own personal journey will take them. We can decide where we'd like to go in life, although there are no guarantees that we'll get there. But what we can do is give ourselves the best chance we can by deciding what the necessary and important things are to get us there, and then doing them.

Any of us might be faced with the kind of major turning points we've heard about this morning. The thing to remember is that a turning point need not be a disaster – it can be an opportunity, a new direction. When you reach your milestones, decide how you can make the most of the opportunities they present. Think of the qualities that *(name your volunteers)* have shown us today, that have helped them follow their chosen journeys.

Handle each milestone properly, and you'll be able to look back and see it as important: an experience you're glad you went through on your own personal journey through life. *(Pause)*

Extra Resources

Alternatively, you could choose as a volunteer someone who has achieved a goal and who has been reported on in the local press.

 ISBN 1 874050 39 2

Theme/ Key value

Journeys

Valuing progress and achievement

Title

From country to country

Summary

This assembly asks students to consider changes of direction in their lives in comparison with the plight of refugees and asylum seekers. It aims to help them gain a sense of perspective when making important decisions.

Resources

Optional Two pre-prepared volunteers to read the extracts.

REFLECTION

■ ***Optional*** *Adapt the first sentences if you are not using the theme as a whole.*

In this theme we're thinking about journeys. Specifically, we're using the idea of a journey as a metaphor for our lives. We're thinking about the paths that our lives take, the milestones we reach and pass through, and the choices we make to determine the directions we go in. In this assembly we're going to think about more literal journeys – ones in which people are physically travelling. But as you hear about these people, think about how the literal journeys they have taken have affected their life journeys.

Sometimes, as part of their life journeys, people decide to leave the country of their birth and move to another one. People emigrate for all kinds of reasons – perhaps to be closer to their relatives, or maybe to go to a new job. But if you emigrate, it's because you choose to take a turning, a new direction to improve your journey through life.

For millions of people these days, however, moving to a new country is a necessity forced upon them by the desperate conditions in their own region, caused by famine, war or persecution. There are many, many children and adults all over the world fleeing from their homes on foot, with no idea where they're going to or where their next meal is coming from. These people are called 'refugees' – they are looking for refuge or shelter. There are 20 million refugees across the world and half of them are children.

■ *Use your community/town/city population to show how great a number 10 million is.*

In 1992, thousands of refugees flooded into Kenya to escape civil wars in Somalia and Sudan. Among them was a boy called Chol. In three years, he travelled 2000km on foot (the equivalent of walking from London to Rome), crossing from Sudan first to Ethiopia and finally to Kenya. Here's part of his story.

■ ***Optional*** *Student 1 reads the story.*

“We were playing at about 5 o'clock when soldiers came. We just ran. We didn't know where we were going to, we just ran. My brother helped me to run. We didn't know where our mother or father were. When there is shooting you don't think about your friend or your mother, you just run to save your life. I didn't see the soldiers, I just heard the shooting and the bombing. It all just happened, like an accident, and we ran without anything – no food, no clothes, nothing.

In the day the sun is hot and your feet burn. So we walked at night when it is cold, because then you don't say all the time, ' I want water, I want water'. To rest we stood under trees, but you can die of hunger if you give up and just lie under a tree. Wild animals, lions, killed many people.

We ate soil and the leaves of trees. The big boys knew the way. I think God showed us the way. He says, 'Go this way,' to the good people. We never felt well. We just walked. People died of hunger. Even my friend

 ISBN 1 874050 39 2

died. I had to leave my friend because I would die with him. When he won't go on, what can you do?"

Chol eventually found his way to a refugee camp in Kenya, housing 40,000 people of whom 25,000 were children. Most of them had no idea where their parents were.

Sometimes, people escaping persecution in their own country can travel out by car or by plane. They are unlikely to die of hunger on their journey, but they still have an extremely hard time. For example, countries who want to discourage large numbers of refugees coming in will insist that you have a visa from your own country allowing you to travel. To get a visa you need a passport, but these are issued by the very authorities you're trying to escape from. If you travel without a visa or passport, you can be immediately returned to your home country.

That's what happened to a young man called Lago. He grew up in the part of Africa called the Ivory Coast. Before 1990, there was only one political party and everyone had to support it. As a student, Lago started campaigning for better education. The ruling party got nervous, because Lago's brother-in-law was a friend of the President and they were afraid Lago might know about some of the government's injustices and start talking about them. Here's part of Lago's story.

■ ***Optional*** *Student 2 reads the story*

"We supported some students who were on hunger strike and the next thing was that my employer was told to dismiss me. I went to live with my brother, but they arrested him secretly. Fortunately, one of his friends warned me to seek refuge elsewhere or I should have been arrested too. Torture is commonplace in the prisons and there are people who have simply 'disappeared'.

I decided to go to Britain because you don't need a visa as you do in France. But unfortunately the plane was in a bad state and had to stop at Nairobi for repairs. This meant that instead of a one-hour transit stop in France, I missed my connecting plane and had to stay overnight. When I got to Britain I was told I would have to seek asylum in France because that was the first 'safe country' I'd stopped at. I didn't have a visa for France, so they would send me back to my own country and to prison. I was told I could appeal against British immigration's decision, so that is what I decided to do.

I was put in a detention centre for six months. There were cameras and loudspeakers everywhere, and your room was searched constantly. Some of us went on hunger strike for better treatment. After six months, they moved me to prison. I don't know why. I got out on £5000 bail. It was paid by a newspaper whose reporter had befriended me during the hunger strike. I've been staying with a journalist and his family since my release. It is nearly a year since I left my country. I've received no letters from my family. I worry most of all about them."

RESPONSE

Commitment and action

So, we've heard about people journeying by force of circumstances from country to country. *(Pause)* Evacuees, refugees, asylum seekers. Imagine how that has affected their life journeys. I'm sure that's not how they originally saw their path through life, and they will have no idea what direction they will have to take next.

None of us are likely to find ourselves making an enforced journey to a new country. But one day you might find yourself forced by circumstances to take a dramatic change of direction in your life journey. Perhaps knowing how people like Chol and Lago have suffered on their journeys will help you to adapt to yours.

Extra Resources

Wilkes, S (1994) *One day we had to run!* London: Evans. Davies, W (1995) *Closing the borders.* Hove: Wayland. Warner, R (1996) *Refugees.* Hove: Wayland.

Theme/ Key value

Journeys

Valuing progress and achievement

Title

Rites of passage

Summary This assembly shows how the major religions' rites of passage and pilgrimage sites stand as patterns for those who want their life journeys to include a spiritual quest.

Resources Four students to read the statements.

REFLECTION

■ ***Optional*** *Adapt the first sentences if you are not using the theme as a whole.*

If it's true – as we have suggested in this theme – that life is like a journey, you'd expect to find that the world's great religions and systems of belief would include something of this 'journey' idea. And indeed they do.

There are similarities between the way that some of them include this idea, too. Many of them use the idea of life as a journey which moves through a series of important events that happen at certain times. The idea is that these are like different milestones that you pass on your way to your final destination. These milestones are sometimes called 'rites of passage' because they are events that mark the main stages you come to on your way through life – birth, growing up, becoming an adult and death.

Such rites of passage are often celebrated by some sort of traditional ritual or ceremony. These four students are going to give us some examples of the ways in which different faiths mark these milestones.

Reader 1: When a new born Muslim baby has been washed, the father or a prayer leader whispers prayers into each of the baby's ears. Then, when the baby gets home, a date, some honey or a small piece of sugar is put in the child's mouth and another prayer is said. Seven days after the baby has been born, there's a special ceremony called 'Aqiqa'. The baby's head is shaved, which symbolises the removal of all misfortune. The hair is weighed, and gold or silver of the same weight is given to the poor. If the baby is a girl, a sheep or a goat is killed. If the baby is a boy, two animals are killed. The meat is cooked and one third is given to the baby's relatives and two thirds is given to the poor. Also at this time, the baby is given a name.

Reader 2: A Jewish boy's 13th birthday is when he's considered to have reached adulthood, and so is old enough to take on the religious responsibilities that are expected of adults. This is marked by a ceremony called a 'Bar Mitzvah' which means 'Son of the Commandment'. During a meeting at the synagogue, the boy reads in Hebrew from the Jewish scriptures, which is a privilege preserved for men only. He also receives a special blessing from his father. Communities of Reform and Liberal Jews allow girls to read from the scriptures once they've reached the age of twelve – she then becomes a 'Bat Mitzvah' or 'Daughter of the Commandment'. In the more Orthodox communities girls still have their Bat Mitzvah but aren't allowed to read from the scriptures. Whatever ceremony takes place there's a great party afterwards!

Reader 3: For Christians, the marriage of a man and a woman is seen as a reflection of the relationship between Jesus Christ and the whole Church. The expectation is that the marriage

 ISBN 1 874050 39 2

will be for life. The couple marry by making promises to each other and by giving and receiving rings, which symbolise eternity, because they don't have a beginning or an end. The ceremony is witnessed by other Christians and overseen by a minister.

In the Orthodox Church the couple are also crowned with garlands or coronets, drink wine from the same cup and are led in a circular procession by the priest to symbolise the eternal nature of the marriage.

Reader 4: In the Hindu tradition, when a person dies, the body is taken on the same day to an open-air cremation ground and covered with sweet-scented wood. The eldest son, or another close relative, walks three times round the funeral pyre and pours holy water over the body. He then puts a flame to the wood, with some special words asking that the dead person's shortcomings may be burned and that the person may 'attain the shining regions'. Hindus believe in re-incarnation – they believe the soul lives on after death and is re-born in a new body. This means the body is not needed after death, which is why it is cremated.

In the West, where a Hindu is usually cremated in a crematorium, the ashes are often collected and sent to India to be scattered on the river Ganges.

■ *Thank the readers and continue.*

Think of your own lives for a moment. In your own ways, you will all have taken part in some of those 'rituals'– those milestones we've just heard about. And, as you continue on your journey through life, you will take part in others – new babies, eighteenth birthdays, weddings, funerals and so on.

Most of these you will celebrate publicly in some way too – celebration is an important part of reaching milestones. Why do you think people get together and make a special occasion about these things?

Well, milestones, as we have said, often mark the achievement of a new stage in life, or the making of an important decision. And when this happens the ceremonies that celebrate them – to name a baby, or Bar Mitzvahs for example, or weddings – allow all the people involved publicly to reaffirm and show their values and beliefs which play an important part in achieving those milestones. The celebration, or 'rite', says 'these are the things we believe in – this is a special moment to stop and remind ourselves about what is really important.'

RESPONSE

Commitment

Milestones are important because they mark the points where we take stock of our lives and decide where we are going next.

Suppose you were going to plan a rite of passage, or celebration, for yourself as you move into the adult part of your life. What are the qualities, the values and the beliefs you would want to show people? *(Pause)*

You probably need some time to think about that. But it is something that's worth thinking about. People who have a good idea of what values they've chosen are like a ship with a rudder – the values help steer them through their journey through life. People who don't bother are like a ship without a rudder – at best they drift, at worst they are out of control and will hit the rocks.

Extra Resources

Keene, M (1993) *Seekers after Truth – Hinduism, Buddhism, Sikhism.* Cambridge: Cambridge University Press. Keene, M (1993) *Believers in One God – Judaism, Christianity, Islam.* Cambridge: Cambridge University Press.
Teaching about World Faiths: curriculum support for teachers. (1995) Essex County Council Education.

pfp, 61 Gray's Inn Road, London WC1X 8TL ISBN 1 874050 39 2

Theme/ Key value

Journeys

Valuing progress and achievement

Title

The excitement of journeying

Summary

This assembly uses real examples of concern being shown for young people at a turning point in their lives and suggests that we have some control over the directions we take.

Resources

Supplied OHT image (p96).

REFLECTION

Today we hear the advice that was given by two adults to young people who were at a turning point in their lives. First, listen to this section of a letter that the novelist Fay Weldon wrote to her niece Alice.

❝The last time I saw you, you were two, blonde and cherubic. Now, I gather, you are eighteen, you dye your hair black and green and your mother, my sister, is perturbed. I shall not interfere between the two of you: I shall confine myself to the matters you raise...

You tell me, in passing, that you are doing a college course in English Literature, and are obliged to read Jane Austen; that you find her boring, petty and irrelevant and, that as the world is in crisis, and the future catastrophic, you cannot imagine what purpose there can be in your reading her.

My dear child! My dear, pretty little Alice, now with black and green hair.

How can I hope to explain Literature to you, with its capital 'L'? You are bright enough. You could read when you were four. But then, sensibly, you turned to television for your window on the world: you slaked your appetite for information, for stories, for beginnings, middles and ends, with the easy tasty substance of the screen. You lulled yourself to sleep with visions of violence, and the cruder strokes of human action and reaction; stories in which every simple action has a simple motive, nothing is inexplicable, and even God moves in an un-mysterious way.

And now you realise this is not enough: you have an inkling there is something more, that your own feelings and responses are a thousand times more complex than this tinny televisual representation has ever suggested: you have, I suspect and hope, intimations of infinity, of the romance of creation, of the wonder of love, of the glory of existence; you look around for companions in your wild new comprehension, your sudden vision, and you see the same zonked-out stares, the same pale faces and dyed cotton-wool hair, and you turn, at last, to education, to literature, and books – and find them closed to you.❞

(Pause) You may have noticed that Fay Weldon did not actually give Alice any real advice at all – no explicit reasons why she should read Jane Austen. But the reasons why Alice found her irrelevant, and the reasons why deep down she now needed something more emotionally and mentally satisfying than TV, were all there in the letter, if Alice was prepared to see and hear them.

Now here's part of a talk given some years ago by a head teacher to students who were about to leave school.

❝An awful lot of grown ups spend an awful lot of time complaining about their own lives, how uninteresting their lives are, how dull their jobs are, how small their pay is, how unreliable their cars, how tasteless their food.

Well, all this may be true, but if they are complaining to other people, and invariably they do, they are complaining to the wrong person. They should be complaining to themselves, for they themselves are to blame.

Our lives are what we make of them, and if they are dull and uninteresting, frustrated, colourless and unsatisfying, it is because we have made them so.

It is no good blaming those mysterious people 'they' at whose door we like to lay so many of our misfortunes.

So what must we do to lead full and fruitful lives about which we will not wish to complain?

 ISBN 1 874050 39 2

The first thing (and this is the first step in being really grown-up) is to understand that our lives are what we make of them, and that for most of us the credit for a good life is ours, just as the blame for a bad life is ours also.

The second thing is to know ourselves. We are not all the same, we are all different. We have not all got the kind of mind that makes a scientist, or the kind of sensitivity that makes an artist, or the co-ordination and quick reactions that make a fine sports player. But there is no-one who has not got qualities, gifts and talents of one sort or another, and we must find out and know what our own talents are.

The third thing we must do if we are to lead full and fruitful lives is to be ourselves. It is astonishing how few people have the courage and self-confidence really to be themselves. Yet, unless they are, they can never have full, fruitful and happy lives; for a full, fruitful and happy life is a life of self-fulfilment, a life in which the qualities, gifts and talents we possess and which are our own, are developed and used to the full.

So many people spend their time and energy trying to be somebody else. Be yourself, and you will be a much better person than you will ever be by trying to be someone else. Know yourself and, with God's help, fulfil the nature of your own being; be yourself.”

(Pause) Perhaps Alice had got to the point where she was beginning to suspect just that – that our lives are what we make of them. She was obviously intelligent, but she needed to feed that intelligence with the right material.

We're not all cut out to do English Literature at college. We've all got different gifts and talents, as that head teacher pointed out. We should try to find out what we are cut out for, and go for it. Know yourself, he said, and be yourself.

■ ***Optional*** *Adapt the following paragraph if you are not using the theme as a whole.*

We are all at different stages of our journeys through life, and we've seen throughout this theme of 'Journeys' that there's no way of knowing where our life journey will take us. It makes good sense to define some kind of destination, and to do what we think is required to get there. But we've also seen that life has a habit of throwing up barriers and turning points. You could finish up at an entirely different destination, and be very happy to be there.

RESPONSE

Commitment

■ *Show supplied OHT image.*

Life is a journey full of excitement and possibilities. You have already started on your journeys, and there is a long road ahead of you yet. You will make some decisions now, but may well take a different direction later on. Whatever you choose, make your choices carefully and courageously to make the most of all the possibilities that your journey will throw at you.

■ ***Optional*** *Adapt the next paragraph if you have not used the theme as a whole.*

Where do you think you'll be ten years from now? What's along the road for you? What will be the next turning point on offer? Will you take a new direction, or persevere with your earlier choice? Think about those questions again as I read again the poem we had at the beginning of these assemblies.

I am being driven forward
Into an unknown land
The pass grows steeper
The air colder and sharper
A wind from my unknown goal
Stirs the strings
Of expectation.

Extra Resources

The Fay Weldon extract is from *Letters to Alice* (Penguin) and quoted in Thomson, J (1991) *Many Thoughts*, London: Hodder & Stoughton. The head teacher extract is adapted from *The Aiglon Meditation*, (1989), Canterbury Aiglon College, Switzerland. The poem is by Dag Hammarskjöld, published in *Markings* (London: Faber and Faber, 1964) and reproduced with kind permission.

Theme

Peace

Assemblies on this theme

1 'Peace be with you'
This assembly introduces the theme of peace and explores the concept of shalom. It requires some preparation.

2 Pacifism
This assembly uses a 'line discussion' to explore some of the issues of pacifism. It is probably most effective in a year group assembly or in separate Key Stage 3 and Key Stage 4 assemblies. It requires some preparation.

3 Making peace
This assembly discusses peace as a process rather than a product and asks students to consider their role as 'peacemakers' in their own lives.

4 'I don't want to be afraid'
This assembly uses direct quotations from students in Northern Ireland to describe the meaning of the word peace in relation to the situation those students face in their daily lives. It aims to enable students to realise that there are young people in Britain who do not live in peace and security as the majority do. It requires some preparation.

5 Peace of mind
This assembly brings together some of the ideas of the previous assemblies in this theme. It asks students to find the positive 'peaceful' aspects of their school community with an emphasis on the notion of peace as 'freedom from anxiety'. It concludes with a commitment to making the school community a more peaceful place (or a continuing peaceful place) through individual action. It requires some preparation. .

Record of use

Taken by	1	2	3	4	5
Date					
Given to					

Comments

pfp, 61 Gray's Inn Road, London WC1X 8TL May be photocopied for use within the purchasing institution only.
 ISBN 1 874050 39 2

‘Let there be peace in our school and let it begin with me.’

pfp, 61 Gray’s Inn Road, London WC1X 8TL ISBN 1 874050 39 2

Theme/ Key value

Peace

Respect for the rights of others

Title

'Peace be with you'

Summary

This assembly introduces the theme of peace and explores the concept of shalom. It requires some preparation.

Resources

A CD of a peaceful piece of music. A colleague and/or student to read the quotations. ***Optional*** Another colleague who was a student in the 60s or 70s.

REFLECTION

■ *Begin the assembly by playing the CD. After about 2 minutes of music, start talking but continue music playing in background.*

This is a nice way to *(start/end)* the day – very peaceful and quiet. I wish all our time at school was like this! *(Pause)*

But is this really peaceful? Does it really make me feel full of peace? Hmmm... I'm still feeling cross about the person who pulled out in front of my car *(or use your own scenario)* this morning and I have a list of students to deal with for non-arrival of homework *(again, use your own scenario)*. Neither of those things makes me feel peaceful.

So, is peace just the absence of noise? Can you make peace just by being quiet and turning on some nice, calm music?

Let's think for a minute about what peace actually is.

■ *Turn off the music.*

Reader: 'It is peace until the rising of the dawn.'

Leader: So peace is what happens while we're asleep...

Reader:

I will arise now and go to Innisfree
And a small cabin build there, of
  clay and wattles made;
Nine bean rows will I have there, a
  hive for the honey bee,
And live alone in the bee-loud glade.
And I shall have some peace there, for
  peace comes dropping slow...

Leader: And peace is what we can achieve by being on our own...

■ ***Optional*** *You might choose a colleague or different reader to say the following paragraph.*

Reader: Peace, man! I was a student in the 60s/70s when 'peace' was a frequent greeting. Peace then was about dropping out, wearing flowers in your hair, demonstrating against war and the nuclear bomb and loving everyone who would let you! And being with other people who were just like yourself.

Leader: So, peace is also what is achieved by caring for others and doing things together.

Let me tell you about a place where two buildings give us a great insight into the idea of peace.

At Eynsford in Kent, a couple of miles from the car race track at Brands Hatch, there are two historic sites which you can visit. One is a Roman villa which was built in a time of peace, when people could enjoy life. It has underfloor heating, an open courtyard with a pool and beautiful mosaic floors. It all gives evidence of a peaceful way of life – there must have been other villas in the area and the wealthy family who lived there didn't need high walls, or weapons to defend themselves. This was a house in a Roman Britain that was at peace. It was a place designed to welcome people in, not keep them out. It also had an early Christian chapel in its grounds.

 ISBN 1 874050 39 2

Just half a mile up the road are the remains of a fortress. It was an imposing structure with massive defences all round it. Inside was a great draughty hall with small bare bedrooms off to the sides. The kitchens were quite a walk from the hall where everyone ate together. There was little natural light because this was a defensive building, with small slit windows through which arrows could be shot at advancing enemies.

If you saw these two sites you'd think that Eynsford Castle was built centuries before Lullingstone Roman Villa – but you'd be wrong. The castle was Norman and built about 900 years ago and the Roman villa is about 1,800 years old. The peace of one contrasts with the warring society of the other.

Think about those different definitions of peace while you listen to this Hindu prayer. It was written a very long time ago – somewhere around 700–300 BC.

Reader: Lead me from death to life, from falsehood to truth
Lead me from despair to hope, from fear to rest.
Lead me from hate to love, from war to peace.
Let peace fill our heart, our world, our universe.

This prayer shows what we discovered at the start of this assembly. That peace is many things but, importantly, it isn't just the absence of bad things – war, despair, hate. To have peace, we also need the presence of good things – life, truth, hope, rest, love.

Jews have a special word for this kind of peace – peace which is full of good things. That word is 'shalom'. It means being able to be with other people who are different from you and to be in harmony with them, rather than fighting over your differences.

Many religious people believe that such peace can only come from God – that without God we are unable to stop fighting each other and wanting to put ourselves first. That in the presence of God we can stop acting as though everyone else is the enemy and become peaceful – and learn to respect other people and to live in harmony with them.

RESPONSE

Commitment

Whether or not you have a faith, that is still a way of life you can appreciate and aim for. Think about how much calmer and happier life is if you live in harmony with others, rather than fighting over your differences. If you live in peace, in harmony – if your life is full of 'shalom' .

■ ***Optional*** *Include the next paragraph if you are using this theme as a whole.*

Let's think about that this week, and at the end of the week we can assess how 'peaceful' we have managed to make our school community. Not just how quiet it has been (although that would be nice too!) but how full of 'shalom'.

Thoughtfulness

All faiths and belief systems from the Humanist to the Christian have prayers or thoughts about peace. Here's one such prayer which is said by Muslims at the end of Salat.

■ ***Optional*** *A Muslim student could repeat the prayer in Arabic if this is appropriate.*

O God thou art peace. From thee is peace and unto thee is peace. Let us love, our Lord, in peace
and receive us in thy paradise, the abode of peace.

Extra Resources

'Maybe it is only peaceful' is from the Qur'an 97:5. The poem 'I will arise now…' is by WB Yeats, *The Lake Isle of Innisfree*. The Hindu prayer is adapted from the *Upanishads*. The final prayer is the close of formal Muslim prayers.

Theme/ Key value

Peace

Respect for the rights of others

Title

Pacifism

Summary

This assembly uses a 'line discussion' to explore some of the issues of pacifism. It is probably most effective in a year group assembly or in separate Key Stage 3 and Key Stage 4 assemblies. It requires some preparation.

Resources

About 20 students. They need to include some pacifists, some who believe that war/fighting is the best way to settle problems, and some who believe that peace is best but fighting is sometimes necessary. They will need to be prepared in advance as they will be asked to justify their stance. A line made with tape, a rope, or something similar running across the front of the stage.

REFLECTION

Albert Einstein once said: 'I am an absolute pacifist… It is a feeling that possesses me, because the murder of men is disgusting.'

I wonder how many of you have thought about pacifism? It's one of those issues that's not as straightforward as it may seem at first.

Pacifism takes a variety of forms. But, basically, pacifists want to show that evil cannot be conquered by evil means and that non-violent policies and actions can be powerful instruments in human affairs.

This requires that people who are pacifists must have great inner strength and be sure of their beliefs. Taking a non-violent stance against people who are taking a violent one towards you isn't easy.

One of the most striking examples of a person promoting non-violence in the modern world was Mahatma Ghandi, who used peaceful means to help drive the British out of India in the 1940s. He in turn had a very strong influence on the thoughts and actions of Martin Luther King Junior in the United States. King was a powerful speaker, a passionate Christian and civil rights campaigner. He once said, 'Through violence you may murder the hater, but you do not murder hate.'

But non-violent methods have proved very hard to apply. The civil rights movement in the United States met with very violent reactions and Martin Luther King was killed by an assassin's bullet.

The issue of pacifism has long been debated. Although some Christians are pacifists, many others do believe in the idea of a 'just' war. The war must have the intention of establishing a good or correcting an evil, it must be waged by acceptable means and it must be aimed at a just peace. There are other conditions in Christian writings for a just war, but they all raise questions about things like the use of nuclear weapons, modern wars of liberation and guerilla warfare and terrorism. And so far no-one has come up with any answers!

Now let's see what some of you think.

- *Bring the student group up onto the stage and ask them to sit for a moment.*

As you can see, there's a line drawn across this space here. Anyone standing at this end *(move to one end of the line)* believes that you should never, ever fight anyone. At the other end (*move to the other end of the line)* are those who believe that fighting is usually the best way to settle an argument. In the middle *(move to the middle of the line)* they think that it depends on the circumstances whether you should fight someone or whether you should try and find a peaceful solution to your conflict. At other points on the line are positions in between those three.

pfp, 61 Gray's Inn Road, London WC1X 8TL ISBN 1 874050 39 2

■ *Address the student group.*

Now, would you please go and stand where you think you are on the line…

■ *Ask several of the students to justify their position on the imaginary line.*

Now I am going to read out several situations. If any of these people change their mind after hearing them – if they think that in that situation they would act differently – they can change their position on the line.

Situation number one. It is the First World War. You have a wife and children. You have been called up to join the army. Many people you know have already gone, and some have been killed or seriously injured. You will be fighting for your country. Do you go?

■ *Wait to allow anyone to move.*

Situation number two. You live on a housing estate where a gang of teenagers has been destroying property and frightening everyone. The situation has now got completely out of control and the estate has even become a no-go area for the police. A group of your neighbours decide to form a vigilante group to protect their property and families. Do you join?

■ *Wait to allow anyone to move.*

Okay, situation number three. You are a single woman student. There have been several brutal attacks on women on the university campus, including one on a good friend of yours. You are very frightened, but at the same time refuse to become a prisoner in your flat, too scared to go out in the evening. A friend offers to lend you a small gun to carry, 'Just so you feel safe'. Do you accept?

■ *Wait to allow anyone to move.*

Finally, situation number four. You live in Northern Ireland, and feel strongly committed to a certain cause. You suspect that one of your friends belongs to a paramilitary organisation which supports the same cause. One day he asks you to join his group. He explains that you may need to use violence on occasions to achieve the aims of the group. Do you join?

■ *Wait to allow anyone to move.*

■ ***Optional*** *Discuss with individuals and with the group why students may have changed position in different situations.*

RESPONSE

Commitment

I wonder where you would have stood on this line – and whether you would have moved?

There are many different situations, and many different opinions. Some people feel more strongly about some things than about others. In this school we try to respect the range of beliefs we have and the range of opinions.

But something else we do is share a commitment to trying to live in peace with each other, and with others in the wider community. Those problems we have just discussed are unusual and extreme, and there is a continuing debate on the rights and wrongs of solving them.

But we don't believe that violence is the way to solve the problems we come up against in our community. In most of these situations violence is the easy option, and doesn't solve anything in the end. Next time you're faced with conflict, meet the challenge by seeing if you can find a peaceful way to reach peace – and to reach it for good. *(Pause)*

Extra Resources

The Einstein quote comes from an interview with Paul Hutchinson in *Christian Century:* 28th August 1929. The paragraphs on pacificism and a 'just' war are adapted from pp 292–293 of *The Lion Handbook of Christian Belief* (1982). Lion Publishing, Tring.

Theme/ Key value

Peace

Respect for the rights of others

Title

Making peace

Summary

This assembly discusses peace as a process rather than a product and asks students to consider their roles as 'peacemakers' in their own lives.

Resources

Nothing at all.

REFLECTION

■ ***Optional*** *Adapt this first paragraph if you are not using this theme as a whole.*

As you know, we're thinking about peace at the moment. We've thought about what peace is, and people's attitudes to it. But how do we actually get peace? How does it happen?

Let's think about a situation that I'm sure we're all familiar with for a moment – friends and enemies. They're usually very different groups of people. You love one group, you hate the other. It seems simple… but it isn't always. Sometimes it's a bit more complicated. Here's a short story, based on real people, that may remind you of your own past and it's about friends becoming enemies and then… well, see what happens.

“Dionne and Kerry had started primary school together and immediately got on like mad. From the first day they had sat together, played together, spent their breaks together and just had fun. As they grew older their friendship continued and they spent hours with each other outside school. They had other mates, but the bond between them was stronger than anything else.

Dionne was the quieter one of the two and she had a more serious side to her than Kerry. Kerry was skinny, never sat still, got into trouble, was bright but lazy, happy-go-lucky and always ready to do anything for her best friend. She'd go 100 miles and stand in the rain to meet Dionne.

Dionne was a good influence on Kerry – she stopped her getting into real trouble sometimes, she encouraged her to do some serious school work at least once a term and she 'looked after' her, a bit like an older sister, when she needed it.

And Kerry was a good influence on Dionne. She brought her out of herself, helped her get a sense of proportion and not take life too seriously. The fun, sunny side of Dionne came out most when she was with Kerry. She'd go 100 miles and stand in the rain to meet Kerry.

But towards the end of primary school things began to go wrong. Kerry joined a dance group and excelled. Dionne went along and tried but she wasn't built for dancing at that level. She belonged to a local church that had lots of music and she got involved with the band that played there every Sunday.

Like all relationships the two girls needed time together and they weren't getting it. They began to drift apart and each blamed the other. When they met now it was strained and they began criticising each other and bickering. On transfer to secondary school, Kerry went to a school that specialised in performing arts and Dionne went to her local school. As they saw each other less and less, they both felt let down and rejected. And to cover their guilt for not keeping in touch, they began to blame each other.

Then, one November evening, Dionne was walking home with some new friends when they saw some girls from Kerry's school hanging out by a cafe. Dionne's group were all in school uniform while the girls from the other school could wear what they wanted. It was an insignificant difference really, but enough to cause friction.

The group outside the cafe started yelling across the road at Dionne and her mates, calling them everything under the sun, because they looked different. Dionne's group shouted back with insults that were just as vicious. Then it happened – Dionne saw Kerry screaming across at her and Kerry saw Dionne,

pfp, 61 Gray's Inn Road, London WC1X 8TL ISBN 1 874050 39 2

standing alone to the side of her friends. All the frustrations and disappointments of their failed friendship came to the surface in both girls. They were enemies.

They didn't speak or see each other at all after that. Both of them got on and pretended they didn't care – although they did. They had grown up together, done everything together, and now, although neither of them would admit it, they missed each other terribly.

About a year later, Dionne's parents were planning a 14th birthday party for Dionne, for family and friends, and Kerry's parents were invited. Together, they came up with a risky plan. Why not try to get Kerry to go too? There would be loads of people there and perhaps, just perhaps, they could begin to re-build their friendship and make peace with each other.

At the beginning of the party the atmosphere was somewhat strained. Kerry on one side of the room and Dionne on the other – both talking to everyone except each other. But gradually, as the evening went on, they were kind of drawn to each other. It became obvious that you couldn't be in the same room as your oldest friend and not talk. And besides, they hadn't seen each other for so long there was a lot to talk about.

The party didn't solve everything. They had a good time, and agreed to meet the next day. But that turned into a huge row. All the bitterness and anger of the last couple of years came out, and they said some pretty mean things to each other. But they also said that they'd missed each other. and that it was because they liked each other, so much that they had felt all that hurt and anger.

It was a long process after that. They started to see each other every so often, or would speak on the phone. There would sometimes be more rows – a lot of 'Well, you did this' and 'Only because you did that' went on. But there was a lot of giggling and a lot of fun too. They both realised that what they had between them was valuable and important, and had to last. But they also realised that if it was going to last, they had to make it happen. They had to make the effort. They had to make peace.” *(Pause)*

If you make a loaf of bread you need certain ingredients like flour, water, yeast and salt. Then you have to knead the dough – work on it and shape it. Well, peace has ingredients too. Let's think of some possible ingredients of peace:

- ***Optional*** *Ask students 'What do you think some of the ingredients might be?' and take some answers.*

How about love, forgiveness, harmony, tolerance, respect, care, understanding?

Dionne and Kerry needed all these and some more to become friends again – to make their peace. Because peace doesn't just happen, it does have to be made. But that can be hard work. It needs all those ingredients for it to succeed. Unlike bread you can't just go into a shop and buy peace. It has to be made – it has to be worked at.

RESPONSE

Acknowledging shortcomings and failings

Some of us aren't so good at making peace. We're OK at making sure we keep enemies – if you're like that just think of how you might turn it around and become a bit more of a peacemaker. *(Pause)*

Commitment

Here's an old Celtic prayer that asks us to be committed to making peace. Think how it might apply to us, hundreds of years after it was written.

It is better to roam the world
with a stick in your hand for pulling fruit from trees
Than a sword at your side for killing enemies.
God has put fruit on trees to sustain our bodies,
And love in our hearts to make enemies into friends.

Extra Resources

The prayer is taken from *Celtic Parables* by Robert van de Weyer (1997) SPCK.

pfp, 61 Gray's Inn Road, London WC1X 8TL ISBN 1 874050 39 2

Theme/ Key value

Peace

Respect for the rights of others

Title

'I don't want to be afraid'

Summary

This assembly uses direct quotations from students in Northern Ireland to describe the meaning of the word peace in relation to the situation those students face in their daily lives. It aims to enable students to realise that there are young people in Britain who do not live in peace and security as the majority do. It requires some preparation.

Resources

Eleven pre-prepared readers aged 11 to 13. Give them copies of the assembly beforehand with the passage each is to read clearly marked.

REFLECTION

If you asked people if Britain is at peace, a great many would probably say 'Well yes, of course! Just look around at the cities, towns and villages. Where are the guns? Where are the soldiers? Where are the tanks? The mortars? The bombs? Where are the wounded and the dead?'

And in one way they'd be right – almost all of Britain is at peace. But for some people, of course, this is not true. On a daily basis, they see soldiers and armoured cars on their streets. They have heard the sound of gunfire, the thud of bombs and some of them have experienced the awful feeling of grief at the death or injury of a member of their family or a friend, through violence.

- ***Optional*** *Adapt the following sentence depending on the location of your school: Northern Ireland or elsewhere.*

I'm talking, of course, about Northern Ireland. I'm talking, of course, about here in Northern Ireland.

- *If your school is in England, Scotland, or Wales use the following paragraphs.*

Of course, there are some people outside of Northern Ireland who have also had terrible experiences of violence because of the troubles there – people in Manchester and London, for example, who have suffered in bomb blasts. Many people in our community and in our school will have their own thoughts and beliefs about the rights and wrongs of the situation in Northern Ireland, but today we are thinking solely about peace.

There is no doubt that many young people in Northern Ireland have had some very different experiences to those that young people have had here. It may well be that those experiences have led them to consider – more than we usually have to – what peace really means. Let's hear what peace does mean to them. And, although our students are reading the quotes, as you listen to them please remember that they were written by students in Northern Ireland – young people, the same age as you. This is what they had to say.

- *Go on to the quotes on the next page.*

- *If your school is in Northern Ireland use the following paragraphs.*

The people in our community and in our school have their own thoughts and beliefs about the rights and wrongs of our situation, but I'm sure all of us think about peace. Today we have the opportunity to share our own thoughts about peace with students from another school here in Northern Ireland. This is what they had to say:

pfp, 61 Gray's Inn Road, London WC1X 8TL ISBN 1 874050 39 2

Reader 1: My name is Alan. I am 11 years old. What peace means to me is the Protestants and Catholics would join up and make friends. I think this is just a silly argument over nothing.

Reader 2: My name is Jason. I am 12 years old. I wish the IRA would stop blowing up cars and different things or having bomb scares. I wish we could go to different places in safety.

Reader 3: My name is Robert. I am 12 years old. Peace means to me no more fighting and no more evil. I wish they would stop fighting. Already millions of people in Northern Ireland and other parts of the United Kingdom are dead. I want to go to places without fear of being beaten up.

Reader 4: My name is Derek. I am 12 years old. What peace means to me is when the ceasefire was on. Then the IRA started again and peace was broken.

Reader 5: My name is Robert. I am 12 years old. Peace means a world with nobody arguing or a world that people were not divided or a place where you don't have to be scared.

Reader 6 My name is Lynette. I am 12 years old. Peace means when the IRA and the UVF stop bombing each other. Let them get along with each other and forget that the Protestants and the Catholics have different religions.

Reader 7: My name is Dean. I am 11 years old. What peace means to me is if the IRA and the UVF comes to some agreement to talk in a hall over the troubles through the past. The reason is because it was nice and peaceful with nothing to worry about and people could do their shopping.

Reader 8: My name is Billy. I am 13 years old. Peace means do not fight and do not hurt no one and try to make friends with your enemy.

Reader 9: My name is Padraig. I am 13 years old. All the people want is peace in the country. That means no more shooting and killing and no more trouble all we want is peace, that is not to hard too ask for, it is always going to be like that if it starts.

Reader 10: My name is Michael. I am 12 years old. Peace means no shooting and no fighting and no killings and no more trouble. All we want is peace.

RESPONSE

Thoughtfulness

'All we want is peace.' If you believe in a God you might want to repeat that plea as a prayer. *(Pause)* And if you share our belief in this school that all of us deserve the right to go about our daily lives without fear, then let that thought be a special one for the children and young people of Northern Ireland.

■ ***Optional*** *If your school is in Northern Ireland use the following text:*

'All we want is peace'. If you share our belief in this school that all of us in our different communities deserve the right to go about our daily lives without fear then let that thought be a special thought for today and every day in the future.' *(Pause)*

Extra Resources

Very many thanks to Yvonne Naylor at the Corrymeela Community, Belfast, and Carol Greer and the pupils of the City of Armagh High School. Their contributions and help is much appreciated.
The Corrymeela Community is a group of Christians – both Catholic and Protestant – in Ireland. It was established in 1965 as a community of reconciliation, and is committed to working to heal social, religious and political divisions in Ireland and throughout the world. Their work includes both a schools programme and a youth programme: they can be contacted in Northern Ireland at Corrymeela Community, Corrymeela House, 8 Upper Crescent, Belfast BT7 1NT, and in the UK at Corrymeela Link, PO Box 118, Reading, Berkshire RG1 1SL.

Theme/ Key value

Peace

Respect for the rights of others

Title

Peace of mind

Summary

This assembly brings together some of the ideas of the previous assemblies in this theme. It asks students to find the positive 'peaceful' aspects of their school community with an emphasis on the notion of peace as 'freedom from anxiety'. It concludes with a commitment to making the school community a more peaceful place (or a continuing peaceful place) through individual action. It requires some preparation.

Resources

Supplied OHT image (p108). A list of peaceful events which have happened in school during the course of this theme. You will have needed to collect examples in preparation, for example: students sitting talking quietly during lunchtime; someone showing another student where to go when they were lost in school; a class working quietly (name the lesson); students/colleagues laughing together, and so on. Make sure that as many of the things you note as possible show 'peace of mind', and symbolise a 'freedom from anxiety'.

REFLECTION

■ ***Optional*** *Adapt the first paragraph if you have not used the theme as a whole.*

At the beginning of this week you were asked to think about whether our school community is a peaceful one. Well, I've made a list of 'peaceful things' which have happened this week – and I have been pleasantly surprised to find how many parts of school life are peaceful. Listen to some of these examples:

■ *Read out your list of peaceful events.*

■ ***Optional***
Can you think of any other situations which I have missed from my list that show peace?

■ *Take contributions from students.*

There are a lot of good things about that list we have observed, such as the many peaceful moments of quiet reflection that have occurred. But there have also been demonstrations of peace shown in moments of fun and enjoyment people have had, and what is especially good about that, is that it shows those people have peace of mind. And that is a very important thing to have if we are to make the most of our lives and fulfil our potentials.

Someone in year 7 *(or whatever the lowest year is in your school)* said that when they came to the school they were very frightened because they thought that they would be picked on for being new and not knowing what to do. But they have found out that we are a peaceful community, where people do empathise with each other – that you can still remember what it was like to be new. You might say that student now has 'peace of mind' – what the dictionary describes as a freedom from anxiety. But peace is not just the absence of war or of anxiety or fear – it is the presence of contentment, of shalom.

■ *If you did not do Assembly 1 in this theme you may like to explain the meaning of shalom again.*

It is very important for us as a community that everyone in this school has peace of mind. I know that some of you are anxious or fearful because of what you have done – or not done – and you're the only one who can get rid of that fear. But, generally, we can all make this a place of tolerance and harmony and empathy – a place where we can all have peace of mind – a place of 'shalom'.

Some years ago a young boy called Neil Reid appeared on *Opportunity Knocks*

pfp, 61 Gray's Inn Road, London WC1X 8TL ISBN 1 874050 39 2

which was a TV show for new talent. The song he sang had the following lyrics:

Let there be peace on earth and let it begin with me.
Let there be peace on earth; the peace that was meant to be.
With God as our father, brothers all are we,
Let me walk with my brother in perfect harmony.

Let peace begin with me. Let this be the moment now
With every step I take let this be my solemn vow
To take each moment and live each moment in peace eternally
Let there be peace on earth and let it begin with me.

To be able to make peace we have to have peace inside ourselves. We can't be angry on the inside and then gentle and peaceful on the outside.

Buddhists aim to develop inner peace through meditation. They rid themselves of selfish and impure thoughts, and focus on the development of peace and tranquillity and 'right' actions. The teachings of the Buddha are called the Dhamma. Here's a quote that sums up the aim of the teachings:

'To avoid all evil, to do good, to purify one's mind – that is the teaching of the Buddhas.'

That's not to say that the path to inner peace is an easy one. Mahinda Jinasena is an eleven year old boy in Sri Lanka. This is what he says about the teachings of the Buddha

"...the Buddhist scriptures give me a lot of headaches. At boxing practice in school I like to punch the other boy hard, but the Dhamma tells me not to harm others. I know where my mother keeps the chocolates and I take one or two sometimes, but the Dhamma tells me not to take what is not given.

Although I have not finished my homework, I say that I have so that I can watch television, but the Dhamma tells me not to tell what is not true. This is the difficulty."

So, living up to the teachings of the Buddha isn't easy for Mahinda. It's almost like everyday life keeps getting in the way and presenting him with other options – boxing practice, television...

That sounds quite familiar doesn't it? But still, it seems that Mahinda knows that the scriptures are teaching him something important – the path to inner peace. And for Mahinda, just as for all of us, finding inner peace will enable him to help make and keep peace everywhere else.

RESPONSE

Action and commitment

It's not easy developing inner peace, or working for peace – we have to work very hard as individuals and as a community. Perhaps we can help ourselves to do that by keeping in mind a slightly adapted version of Neil Reid's song:

■ *Show supplied OHT image.*

'Let there be peace in our school and let it begin with me.'

I would like you to look carefully at the OHT, and try not to forget those words. As we said earlier, we can all help to make this a place of tolerance, harmony and empathy – a place where we can all have peace of mind – a place of 'shalom'. Don't you think that sounds like a good place to be?

Extra Resources

The Buddhist quote is from the *Dhammapada*, verse 183. The Mahinda quote is from *Buddhist Scriptures: Anil Goonewardene* (1994) Heinemann.

The song *Let there be peace...* was written by Sy Miller and Jill Jackson (1955) copyright Jan-Lee Music.

 ISBN 1 874050 39 2

Theme

In the news

Assemblies on this theme

1 'Good news'
This assembly looks at how freedom in publishing and the media enables a society to explore issues and seek truth. It uses an extract from a science, fiction story to draw a contrast between a 'free' society and a repressive one.

2 Propaganda
This assembly looks at the power of advertising and the media to manipulate the truth and the danger of 'propaganda'.

3 The many faces of censorship
This assembly looks at the need to be aware of the different forms censorship can take, especially when freedom and truth is challenged.

4 Respect – the privacy principle
This assembly looks at the individual's right to privacy and the need to respect that right. It needs some preparation.

5 'To be or not to be: that is the question'
This assembly looks at the need to keep an open mind and to be aware of the often one-sided viewpoint presented by the media.

Record of use

Taken by	1	2	3	4	5
Date					
Given to					

Comments

pfp, 61 Gray's Inn Road, London WC1X 8TL ISBN 1 874050 39 2

‘Everyone has the right to freedom of opinion and expression; this right includes freedom to hold opinions without interference and to seek, receive and impart information and ideas through any media and regardless of frontiers.’

Article 19 of the United Nations Universal Declaration of Human Rights

pfp, 61 Gray's Inn Road, London WC1X 8TL ISBN 1 874050 39 2

Theme/ Key value

In the news

Valuing truth and keeping an open mind

Title

'Good news'

Summary

This assembly looks at how freedom in publishing and the media enables a society to explore issues and seek truth. It uses an extract from a science fiction story to draw a contrast between a 'free' society and a repressive one.

Resources

There are no resources needed for this assembly.

REFLECTION

There's a lot of truth in the old saying 'You never appreciate what you've got until you lose it!' For example, in our school we have playing fields and tennis courts *(select PE/games facilities appropriate to your school)* and, of course, we take them for granted. But imagine how difficult our sports and PE programme would be if they were suddenly taken away from us – we might have to travel to another area, or lose the chance of enjoying some sports entirely.

And think about something else you'd miss: TV. Almost everyone here will have a TV at home. You can watch your favourite soap every week or even video it while you're out – it's all so easy. But imagine going home tonight and finding that all TVs and videos had been banned by the government. Lorries with huge skips on them are down every street, on every estate, collecting TVs and taking them to be destroyed. I think you'd value and appreciate what you had after that experience.

Some things we take for granted are not as obvious as playing fields and TVs. Our assembly today is about one of these: the freedom of the media. By 'media', we mean all those methods of mass communication such as TV, radio, newspapers, magazines, books and so on. Our media in this country is relatively free. I don't mean by this that we don't pay for it. I mean that it is relatively free to say what it wants.

For example, there are programmes on TV and radio which often set out to uncover uncomfortable truths. (*Use current examples if appropriate.*) They put politicians on the spot, expose corruption or injustice and try to keep us aware and informed so that we can make our own judgements about issues rather than being manipulated by being told only what others want us to know. And we can go to a bookshop tomorrow and buy books about almost anything.

The freedom writers and programme makers have to do their work isn't universal – many countries have strict censorship about what can be written, said or investigated. In the Second World War huge numbers of books were burnt by the Nazis. They decided that if people read certain opinions or facts it might undermine the regime. Books were seen as weapons against the state! Someone who took that idea and made a great story out of it was science fiction writer, Ray Bradbury. He wrote a book which describes a society in the future in which all books are banned and people who possess them are treated as criminals. The main character is a sort of fireman called Montag, whose job is to pour kerosene (a type of petrol) over any illegal books and burn them – a fireman who makes fire! The book is called *Fahrenheit 451* because that's the temperature at which book-paper catches fire and burns. Here's a short extract in which the 'fire brigade' has received a telephone tip-off that a certain house has some books in it.

❝The engine slammed to a stop. Beatty, Stoneman and Black ran up the sidewalk,

pfp, 61 Gray's Inn Road, London WC1X 8TL ISBN 1 874050 39 2

suddenly odious and fat in their fireproof slickers. Montag followed.

They crashed the front door and grabbed at a woman, though she was not running, she was not trying to escape. She was only standing weaving from side to side, her eyes fixed on a nothingness in the wall, as if they had struck her a terrible blow on the head... 'Where are they?' said Beatty.

He slapped her face with amazing objectivity and repeated the question. The old woman's eyes came to a focus on Beatty. 'You know where they are or you wouldn't be here,' she said.

Stoneman held out the telephone alarm card… 'Have reason to suspect attic; 11 No. Elm, City. E.B.'

'That would be Mrs Blake my neighbour,' said the woman, reading the initials.

'All right, men, let's get 'em!'

Next thing they were up in musty blackness, swinging silver hatchets at doors that were, after all, unlocked, tumbling through like boys all rollick and shout....

Always before it had been like snuffing a candle. The police went first and adhesive-taped the victim's mouth and bandaged him off into their glittering beetle cars, so when you arrived you found an empty house. You weren't hurting anyone, you were hurting only things!...

But now, tonight, someone had slipped. This woman was spoiling the ritual...

Books bombarded Montag's shoulders, his arms, his upturned face... The men above were hurling shovelfuls of magazines into the dusty air. They fell like slaughtered birds and the woman stood below, like a small girl, among the bodies...

The books lay like great mounds of fishes left to dry. The men danced and slipped and fell over them. Titles glittered their golden eyes, falling, gone.

'Kerosene!'

They pumped the cold fluid from the numbered 451 tanks strapped to their shoulders. They coated each book, they pumped rooms full of it. They hurried downstairs, Montag staggered after them in the kerosene fumes. 'Come on, woman!'

The woman knelt among the books, touching the drenched leather and cardboard...her eyes accused Montag. 'You can't ever have my books,' she said....

She opened the fingers of one hand slightly and in the palm of the hand was a single slender object. An ordinary kitchen match.

The sight of it rushed the men out and down away from the house... The woman's hand twitched on the single matchstick. The fumes of kerosene bloomed around her... (Then she) reached out with contempt for them all, and struck the kitchen match against the railing.

People ran out of houses all down the street.” *(Pause)*

Fahrenheit 451 talks about fire, cruelty and death, all because of the fear of ideas, of challenge, of freedom. We are a long, long way from that story's bleak view of the future, but we need to remember: 'You never appreciate what you've got until you lose it'. We need to protect our freedoms rather than just accept them.

RESPONSE

Thankfulness

Thankfully, we live in a democracy where there is freedom to communicate information and ideas. Sometimes this can cause scandal and pain, but it can also give pride and hope.

And at the same time that our writers and programme makers have a great deal of freedom in our society to express their opinions in the way they want, this also means that those of us who read those stories and see those programmes, don't have to accept them at face value. We are free to ask questions, too.

That is not only important, it's also good news!

Extra Resources

The extract is adapted from *Fahrenheit 451* by Ray Bradbury published by Grafton Books (1986) and reproduced with kind permission.

Theme/ Key value

In the news

Valuing truth and keeping an open mind

Title

Propaganda

Summary This assembly looks at the power of advertising and the media to manipulate the truth and the danger of 'propaganda'.

Resources There are no resources needed for this assembly.

REFLECTION

I imagine that very few of us here would like to think of ourselves as being easily deceived or even cheated by things we hear or see in the media. We don't want to think of ourselves as gullible, accepting at face value things we read in the newspapers and magazines, hear on the radio or see on the television. We like to think we are in control of our thoughts and our lives.

But we are probably more manipulated than we care to imagine. Why did I buy my particular make of car? Why do so many of you want the same brand of shoes? Given that we are all targeted by advertisers – and apparently we are bombarded by over 1,600 advertising images a day telling us what to buy and how to live – perhaps it's not hard to think of the reasons. Truthfully, we are all manipulated to some degree.

■ ***Optional*** *Give examples of adverts currently on TV, hoardings etc.*

Sometimes this manipulation can be so serious that it becomes propaganda. It is used by those in power to control our thoughts and beliefs about people and situations, including our own. Propaganda is most often used during conflicts between countries but it can be used at other times, too.

During the Second World War the Germans used an extremely well-spoken British man to broadcast apparent 'news' to Britain over the radio. The news spoke of German triumphs and encouraged the British to think of surrendering. After a while, it became so obvious that this was propaganda that the British started making fun of this broadcaster. Because of his accent, they called him Lord Haw-Haw.

But what about the British? Did we go through the whole of the Second World War without using propaganda? Hardly. We devised some very similar stunts to try on the Germans. Both the British and the Germans did whatever they could to destabilise each other's people and way of life. Propaganda and warfare go hand in hand. Wherever there is war, you'll find propaganda close by.

Propaganda can also be used to convince a society that they are stronger, better off or more respected than they actually are. Only recently, one country bought a lot of advertising space in some important newspapers in Britain and around the world. Four, six, eight pages at a time – that's a lot of space, and very expensive. Then they wrote the wording for their pages, not as a straightforward advertisement, but as a series of articles which looked similar to those which appeared elsewhere in the papers. These articles praised the virtue of that country, its people, its products and, above all its President.

The country in question doesn't allow much information from the outside world to enter. No foreign newspapers are on sale there. Some weeks after the advertisements appeared around the world, articles praising the country's President started to appear in the country's own newspapers. These articles

pfp, 61 Gray's Inn Road, London WC1X 8TL ISBN 1 874050 39 2

contained sentences such as *The Sunday Times* recently described President X as an heroic leader, taking his people successfully into the twenty-first century and so on.

Well, you probably don't need me to tell you precisely where in *The Sunday Times* those quotes had appeared. Yes, you're right. They were all in the advertisements the country had written about itself and paid to have inserted into the paper. Here was a case of propaganda being used to persuade the people of this country that their President is seen more favourably than he actually is.

The problem with propaganda is that it deliberately sets out to mislead people, masquerading either as the truth or as a reasonable opinion. But truth and reasonable opinions always have evidence to support them. Propaganda doesn't. Propaganda is basically the careful presentation of lies in order to alter the way people feel or behave.

These examples of propaganda have an important message for us.

Hopefully, we are able to make our judgements about people and events based on reliable information. Sometimes this isn't possible. You hear some gossip at break, it's passed on at lunchtime with an extra twist added to make it a bit more interesting and by hometime it's the gospel truth. But unless this is done with malice there is often no real harm done. When it *is* done deliberately then it is a different matter entirely. It really is worth stopping and thinking about why programme makers, newspapers and so on are telling you something.

RESPONSE

Thankfulness

We're lucky in this country to have many freedoms so that the power of the media is constantly being challenged and our politicians and leaders have a chance to speak honestly, if they choose to do so, on TV, radio and in the press. Let's be thankful for that freedom, but guard it carefully and be aware that there's always some group or individuals who will want to manipulate us for their own ends.

Commitment

Think for a moment about your own approach to the truth – are you manipulative? Do you twist the truth to suit your own ends? Are you open to believing the best you hear rather than the worst?

Being as truthful as we can in our own lives is a big step in recognising truth or distortion or propaganda in the media. So learn to question and have the courage to go against the tide, when your own values tell you something's not fair.

Extra Resources

Hollingworth, M (1986) *The Press and Political Dissent*. London: Pluto Press. Miller, D (1994) *Don't Mention the War: Northern Ireland, Propaganda and the Media*. London: Pluto Press. Wallis, R and Baran S (1990) *The Known World of Broadcast News: International News and the Electronic Media*. London: Comedia/Routledge. Yorke, I (1995) *Television News*. Oxford: Focal Press.

 ISBN 1 874050 39 2

Theme/ Key value

In the news

Valuing truth and keeping an open mind

Title

The many faces of censorship

Summary

This assembly looks at the need to be aware of the different forms censorship can take, especially when freedom and truth are challenged.

Resources

Supplied OHT image (p120).

REFLECTION

No way of governing a country is perfect. We live in a democracy, which has often been described as the least worst form of government in the world. It isn't perfect but there don't, as yet, seem to be many better alternatives which maximise our freedom and involvement in the decisions which affect our own lives.

One of the most important aspects of democracy is that the people who live in it need to be informed. We all have the right to vote on issues or make decisions about different things – of course, that's exactly what living in a democracy is all about. However, there's little point in taking part if we don't know what we are talking about. Think about the following questions.

- Should foxhunting be banned?
- Should we be using nuclear power?
- Should wealthy nations support poor nations?
- Should there be a Royal Family?
- Should Great Britain be a formal member of the European Community?

■ ***Optional*** *Add some of your own if you wish.*

Most of us will have instant opinions on each of these. And I bet we can all talk endlessly about some of them. I often do! But if we are to help make a decision which is binding on all of us we need more than just opinions. We need information. Information is at the heart of a democracy. If we don't have information we can hardly be expected to make an informed decision. If we do have to make a decision without information, it's unlikely to be a reasonable one.

So, here is another question. What would be an effective way of controlling a group of people?

Well, one answer is – deprive them of the information they need to think about before they come to a decision.

■ ***Optional*** *Adapt the following paragraph if you are not using the theme as a whole.*

In our last assembly we talked about propaganda. Propaganda is one of the most insidious ways of denying people information. Why? Because propaganda feeds people the wrong information. The use of propaganda creates a feeling that we are being informed, when what is actually happening is that we are being swamped with inaccurate or hopelessly biased information. We are being allowed access to only one facet of the truth.

So propaganda is a form of censorship. Anything which deliberately denies us access to the truth is an act of censorship.

In some countries, certain newspapers and magazines are simply forbidden, not allowed to be on sale or read by anyone. Television and radio are also strictly controlled. The script of each programme is carefully monitored to make sure that nothing can be heard or seen which has not been approved of by the ruling authorities. In some places, no-one is allowed to meet in the streets in groups of more than two or three, in case discussions become too free-ranging.

 ISBN 1 874050 39 2

Living in Britain – and grumbling about it as we all do – you might find this hard to believe. But this level of censorship is happening now, as I'm speaking to you, somewhere in the world.

If we need an informed population to maintain a democratic society, then censorship is clearly a bad thing, right? Unfortunately, like everything else the situation is more complex than it seems at first. Information is vital, it's true. But it may not be appropriate for everyone to have access to all information. The recent growth of the World Wide Web has brought all of this into focus. If I go onto the Internet this evening I can – with a little effort – probably learn how to make a bomb. I might find out about other ways of hurting people. I can certainly find out about all sorts of anti-social behaviour.

Should I be able to do this so easily? That's a question to which no-one has yet come up with a satisfactory answer. But the fact that information is not regulated on the Net has brought the debate about censorship into sharp focus. There are plenty of people who feel that the dangers of total freedom of information will eventually become much greater than the benefits.

Whatever you think about this, the fact remains that information is important if we want to be free people in a real democracy. So we should be concerned enough to keep censorship to the minimum possible. But we ought also to be concerned to make a positive choice to find out as much as we can. If we don't do that, we are censoring ourselves.

RESPONSE

Thankfulness

We are fortunate in this country in having a great deal of freedom and very little serious censorship of what we say about our politicians and the powerful leaders of our society.

Action and commitment

A way of maintaining that freedom – and helping others gain it – is to understand what our rights are and to fight for them.

- *Show supplied OHT image.*

Read this for a moment. This is article 19 of the United Nations Universal Declaration of Human Rights, which states that

> 'Everyone has the right to freedom of opinion and expression; this right includes freedom to hold opinions without interference and to seek, receive and impart information and ideas through any media and regardless of frontiers.'

Let us spend a moment thinking about this. If you believe in a God, you might pray that more and more people in the world today will be able to claim this right.

 ISBN 1 874050 39 2

Theme/ Key value

In the news – the media

Valuing truth and keeping an open mind

Title

Respect – the privacy principle

Summary This assembly looks at the individual's right to privacy and the need to respect that right. It needs some preparation.

Resources Three prepared students to read the sketch. A television and video. ***Optional*** The statements on p128 on an OHT.

REFLECTION

The readers are standing round the TV and video as if watching it. It is to be a video they have secretly filmed of another class in their year group waiting for the teacher to arrive in the classroom.

Reader 1: Ha! Karen and Alisha talking as usual.

Reader 2: Hey! Did you see that? Carla just barged in and interrupted them.

Reader 3: And she's always going on about not interrupting private conversations. What a hypocrite!

Reader 2: Just wait 'till I tell her.

Reader 1: Don't be an idiot. If we're caught doing this, we are dead.

Reader 3: Look at Stevo! He's noticed the open bag of crisps on that desk. They're obviously not his.

Readers 1 and 2 together *(acting this out):* He looks around. No-one's there. He takes just one and... straight in the mouth!

They all laugh.

Reader 1: Good one, my son!

Reader 3: What a pig though.

All readers freeze.

■ *Thank the readers.*

Just imagine, being watched like that all the time. You are walking down the street and someone is behind you, following you. You are talking to a friend on the street corner and you just know someone is there. You are at home relaxing in front of the television and yet you feel uncomfortable. As you look outside the window, you see someone's eyes staring at you, like a bird of prey, waiting for you to drop your guard and slip.

Wherever you go – and I mean *wherever* you go – you are constantly pestered by people, wanting your photograph and signature, wanting to know information about you that is of no real concern of theirs. Enjoyable? Probably for a short time but after that? I guess not. Fair? Almost certainly not. I would hate not to have some privacy in my life – a place or a period of time that is no one else's but my own.

Does this scenario sound familiar to you? You can probably name a dozen people who have to live their lives like this. People like *(choose appropriate members of the royal family, sports personalities, film or music stars)* are all constantly hounded by the media to reveal more about their private lives to form the next big story.

But what is at issue here? *(Pause)*

Well, clearly it is the question of privacy – the right to it and the invasion of it!

The Oxford dictionary defines privacy as 'being withdrawn from society or public interest; being alone and undisturbed; and avoiding publicity'.

Privacy is important to most of us. It often provides us with a chance to think things through and catch up on some rest. But do we have a right to these times of

pfp, 61 Gray's Inn Road, London WC1X 8TL ISBN 1 874050 39 2

privacy? What do you think? Look at these statements and then I'll read them through one at a time. Put up your hands to any you agree with.

■ ***Optional*** *Display the statements on an OHT.*

- No-one has the right to privacy.
- Public figures (the rich, famous and powerful) have no right to privacy.
- Public figures have some right to privacy.
- Ordinary people (those who are not public figures) have a right to privacy.
- Everybody has a right to privacy.

Somewhere there's a balance between our right to know as much as possible and our right to privacy. You may say that inevitably the rich and famous draw attention to themselves by what they do and have, and that as a result they can't avoid a certain amount of invasion of their privacy – it comes with the status. That's probably true.

You may also say that people who are involved in some sensational story deserve the coverage they get. You might not have much sympathy for people *(use an example here if you wish)* who make mistakes and pay dearly for them. Again that may be a view that carries a certain amount of truth.

But how far should this invasion go? At what point should a person, whoever he or she is and whatever he or she does, be left alone by the media and allowed their right to privacy? *(Pause)*

This is a difficult question to answer because it depends on so many different factors. Maybe one approach would be to apply the principle of respect in all circumstances. This principle recognises differences – how important you are in society will obviously determine how much public attention you receive – but it also safeguards standards. No-one should have to experience invasion of privacy that is disrespectful and inhumane. Everyone has the right to be treated with respect. After all, we all value our privacy and deserve the right to it!

RESPONSE

Commitment

There is a golden rule which underlines all the main religions. It states, 'Do unto others as you would have them do unto you'. It's a general principle, which very much applies to this context. If we value our own privacy, we must value it for others, too. If someone trusts you and tells you something in confidence – you know the sort of thing *(Pause)* – then you have a choice: you can keep that confidence and respect their privacy or you can break that confidence and tell someone else.

If you look at some of our national newspapers – especially the tabloids – they often seem to be invading people's privacy and distorting the truth to make a news story. And even the more serious papers aren't much better sometimes.

We try in our school community to respect each other's right to privacy. If you tell us something in confidence we don't shout it from the stage in the hall.

So, when you're dealing with others – be they family, friends, those in authority or those we come into contact with each day, try and show them respect in terms of their privacy. *(Pause)* If you have faith in a God, you might pray for God's help in applying this principle more in your life.

Theme/ Key value

In the news

Valuing truth and keeping an open mind

Title

'To be or not to be: that is the question'

Summary This assembly looks at the need to keep an open mind and to be aware of the often one-sided viewpoint presented by the media.

Resources Supplied OHT master (p120). ***Optional*** A student to read the passage.

REFLECTION

'To be or not to be: that is the question.' You will have all heard this phrase before. I'm sure you have heard it being used in many different contexts. But what does it mean? Well, in Shakespeare's play – where the phrase originated – Hamlet was torn between whether he should avenge his father's death or not.

He had a choice, but he was unsure in his mind about what he should do. And wherever the phrase is used today, it still revolves around the choices we have, the decisions we must make.

The media – certainly as far as factual programmes go – constantly deals with these issues, presenting first one side of the story then another. 'To be or not to be' – that is the question much of the media encourages us to think about.

This choice forms the heart of our society, our democracy. It is something we value and strive to safeguard, so that every person has the freedom to choose on the basis of the presented facts. For example, the freedom to choose which party they voted for in the 1997 election. It is something we take national pride in.

But there is a downside, too. For just as the media has the ability to present the facts so that we can make our own choices, so it has the ability to limit and even deny the choice, as it expresses its own point of view.

A poignant example is that of the actor who originally played Mark Fowler in *Eastenders*, when the series first started. That actor, David Scarboro, was found dead at the bottom of Beachy Head cliffs on April 27th 1988. He had committed suicide.

His brother, Simon, explained in the *Young Guardian* newspaper that constant harassment from the tabloid newspapers had driven David to take his life. Simon wanted to tell the truth about his brother and why he died. This is what he wrote.

■ ***Optional*** *Ask the student to read the following passage.*

"The truth about David's character and lifestyle was vastly different from the way the tabloids portrayed him. But the truth was never scandalous enough to sell their newspapers. So they suggested he was a 'real life runaway' or 'having an affair with another woman' or into heavy drugs. That's what happened to Mark Fowler.

The saddest thing is the ease with which fans go along with it... Knowing how the public confuse actor with character, [David] worried when Mark Fowler became a racist. David was the complete opposite... The producers agreed that he could leave the series for a while to give him time to think things through. But the Sun announced '*Eastenders* Star in Shock Sacking'. That first lie had a tremendous effect; he felt everybody would believe it – after all, it was in the papers!"

Over the next three years, David appeared several more times in Eastenders. But as he did, his name also appeared in the tabloids, and another lie was told. Each time he became more demoralised and depressed. Listen to what his brother said

pfp, 61 Gray's Inn Road, London WC1X 8TL ISBN 1 874050 39 2

"Two *News of the World* reporters had been harassing him for several weeks. At one stage he had already tried to commit suicide. If David gave them an interview, they'd write a sympathetic article. If not...

On the 31st January 1988, the *News of the World* announced on its front page that David was a 'cocaine addict', a 'zombie', a 'weirdo' and it called him 'Dracula'. It devastated David. He broke down and cried. 'Why do they want to do this to me?' he asked.

When he died, his solicitor was preparing to sue the *News of the World* for libel... But we can't continue the case, because under English Law, a dead person has no reputation to protect. I can't agree. I don't want people to remember my brother as the character the newspapers made him. I want people to know that I feel those newspapers robbed me of a dear brother and friend."

While this is clearly a tragic story, it does underline the unattractive consequence of our democracy. The media has tremendous influence, especially when it comes to making judgements or having opinions. In this case, at least Simon was able to give the public an alternative to the one-sided view of the press, so that people could decide for themselves who they believed. Unfortunately, he was able to give it only after his brother had been driven to take his own life.

But where does it leave us? How do we know what we hear and see in the media is not merely the prejudiced opinion of some editor or newspaper owner who has the power to disseminate his personal views through the content of the news?

If the media has the power to destroy one life, as it did David's, it can also destroy many lives. Prejudice spread over a great distance can affect the lives of many people.

By being constantly aware that the media has a particular point of view we can search for another point of view as well. By applying the 'to be or not to be' question to what we see and hear (especially to news which is controversial), we can keep an open mind and be able to decide for ourselves what we agree with, believe, accept or not!

RESPONSE

Thankfulness

- ***Optional*** *Adapt the following slightly if you have not used this theme as a whole.*
- *Show the supplied OHT.*

Let's look again at the statement in the United Nations Universal Declaration of Human Rights which states that freedom of speech is a basic human right. 'Everyone has the right to freedom of opinion and expression; this right includes freedom to hold opinions without interference and to seek, receive and impart information and ideas through any media and regardless of frontiers.'

We can be thankful that we live in a society that values that right, and so enables us to have a media that gives us the chance to get as much information as we can.

But we can also be thankful for something else. We have also talked this week about the limitations of the media. How it can be used to manipulate people, and ways in which freedom of speech can affect people's lives in a very negative way. As we consume our newspapers or TV programmes or books or magazines, let's all remember that, and let's be thankful for the ability and right we have to have our own viewpoint, to be able to take the information we are given, think about it, and make up our own minds.

Commitment

'You are what you read.' *(Pause)* Think for a moment about this statement, and then consider whether you think you have an open mind about what you read in the papers, hear on the radio and see on the television. If not, it may be time to change.

If you believe in a God, you could pray for God's help as you try to find out and value the truth.

pfp, 61 Gray's Inn Road, London WC1X 8TL ISBN 1 874050 39 2

Theme

Courage

Assemblies on this theme

1 What is courage?
This assembly challenges the conventional response to the word 'courage' and begins to explore the idea of courage being linked to the notion of students standing by their own beliefs.

2 Emotional courage
This assembly uses the story of Christopher Reeve to exemplify the kind of personal courage which fights despair and pain and leads to personal development. It aims to encourage students to find courage in their own lives to face crisies and set-backs.

3 Physical courage
This assembly explores the values that underlie those working in the rescue services and asks students to consider their own attitudes towards physical courage and selflessness.

4 The courage of belief
This assembly tries to help students to find the courage to stand by their beliefs, whatever they may be and in spite of what others around may say.

5 The courage to be yourself
This assembly focuses on some of the mechanisms required in finding the courage to be yourself. Although recommended for KS4 some schools may find it appropriate at KS3 as well.

Record of use

Taken by	1	2	3	4	5
Date					
Given to					

Comments

pfp, 61 Gray's Inn Road, London WC1X 8TL ISBN 1 874050 39 2

COURAGE • OHT

pfp, 61 Gray's Inn Road, London WC1X 8TL ISBN 1 874050 39 2

Theme/ Key value

Courage

Striving for personal development

Title

What is courage?

Summary

This assembly challenges the conventional response to the word 'courage' and begins to explore the idea of courage being linked to the notion of students standing by their own beliefs.

Resources

There are no resources needed for this assembly.

REFLECTION

For the next few days in our assemblies we shall be exploring the idea of courage. Most people have got some idea of what courage is. Most people have displayed courage in their own lives at one time or another. If life ran perfectly smoothly, with no obstacles or crises, there would be no need for courage. But life's not like that. Time and again we're all faced with situations that require personal courage.

This morning we're going to hear two incidents of personal courage involving a boy called David. It's taken from a famous book called *I am David* – it was written in 1965, so some of the language might sound a little dated, but try to ignore that and think about what it's about instead. Here's the first:

❝David just managed to catch sight of the boy, a black-haired boy with spiteful eyes, before he was fully occupied in trying to ward off the blows. It was impossible to get away, for the boy was as big as himself, and to escape would mean hitting back. David shielded his head against the boy's blows and clenched his teeth. The blows began to lose some of their force, and the boy seemed to hesitate.

'So you won't hit back, eh? Scared to fight, I suppose?'

David did not answer, and the boy set about him again but less violently this time – rather as if he felt he had to.

'Use your fists, you young swine!'

'No.'

The boy appeared to have grown tired of striking him, at least for the moment, and David sat up with blood streaming from his nose.

'You seem to enjoy a good hiding. Maybe you like me for giving you one!' The boy's voice was sneering.

David regarded him calmly. 'No, I don't. I hate you – and I'd hate you just as much if it had been any one else you'd hit.'

The strange boy looked astonished. 'Why don't you fight then?' he asked crossly.

'Because if I hit you back, I'd be no better than you. I'd be just as rotten and worthless.'

The strange boy grinned at him, but there was a look of uncertainty about him and his eyes shifted uneasily. 'You're not all there!' he said. 'Who do you think you're talking to?'

'I don't think. I know. I'm talking to someone who likes brute force. And that's why I don't want to talk to you any more.'

With that David jumped up smartly and ran off. ...the strange boy did not follow him: he only shouted, 'Idiot! You're a daft coward!'❞

(Pause) Who do you think showed the most courage – David, who wouldn't fight, or the boy who attacked him? *(Pause)* The story continues some days later. David is washing himself and his clothes in a nearby river and while he's waiting for his clothes to dry he sees some small children playing cowboys and indians nearby. The two boys had locked a girl in a shed and made a fire which had got out of hand.

❝'What shall we do?' shouted one of the boys. 'Run and get Carlo, quick!'

Both the boys were crying. One of them set off in the direction David had come from.

David sprang up and took a step forward. Then he turned round, and grabbing his clothes flung them into the river and jumped in after them. They were now sopping wet again...

pfp, 61 Gray's Inn Road, London WC1X 8TL ISBN 1 874050 39 2

The wall of the shed was not yet burning so fiercely, but the door was a regular bonfire. And all those dry leaves and stalks the roof was made of… he would have to get the girl out before the fire got a proper hold...

By the time he reached the burning shed David could hear voices down by the river, but he had no time to look round. With all the speed he could muster he undid his bundle and took out his knife, picked up his wet clothes and with one hand held his trousers up in front of his nose and mouth. Then he sprang into the blazing fire.

The flames had hardly reached the inside, but it was full of smoke. In the middle of the floor sat the little girl tied to an old chair. The tears were streaming from her eyes, and between fits of coughing she was shouting hoarsely for help.

'Shut your eyes,' David told her. 'And your mouth.' He wound his wet shirt round her face, taking care that she could breathe freely inside it. Then he started cutting through her bonds. The knife was not very sharp, and he had to saw backwards and forwards several times until the cords were cut through at last. The girl rose unsteadily to her feet, pulled the shirt from her face, then stumbled. David just managed to catch her as she fainted.

He wound the shirt about her head again. If he could not carry her through the fire, he would throw her clear. He thought he would be able to manage that before he succumbed to the flames. He was terrified of being burned to death, but perhaps it would be over quickly.

For a split second, David hesitated in front of the raging crackling fire which had been a door. Then he made straight for it.

And then it was all over. He had got through and had the girl with him. There were the two little boys outside and several other people as well. He was overcome with coughing… Then he heard a familiar voice.

'And I said you were a coward! I've never before seen anyone do such a brave thing.'

David recognised the boy who had attacked him. There was a man with him.

'Look,' said the man, 'The roof's caught fire now. We should have been too late, Carlo. If he hadn't been here, Maria would have been lost.'” *(Pause)*

For courage to really mean something it has to have a purpose and be linked to some idea of what you believe in. For David the little girl's life was so valuable it was worth risking his life in order to attempt to save her. Doing something just to impress your mates may show a sort of reckless courage, but it's really only for you and is pretty worthless.

Of course, it took a lot of courage for David to rescue Maria from the fire. He was certainly no coward. So why wouldn't he fight Carlo? *(Pause)* Remember what he said to Carlo? He said, 'If I hit you back, I'd be no better than you are.' Let's just think about that for a moment. *(Pause)*

RESPONSE

Action

Think for a minute how you would cope if friends and people around you were to pressure you to do something you don't want to, or don't believe in. Perhaps some of you have found yourself in that situation. You're pressured not to work hard because it's not cool to do so, but you really want to get your qualifications. You're pressured to join in some bullying, when you know that it is cruel to the person being bullied.

It takes courage to put aside your own feelings when someone needs you. It takes courage to do your own thing and not be exactly the same as everyone else. It takes courage to stand up for what you value and believe in.

Do you have that courage?

■

Extra Resources

Holm, A (1991) *I am David.* Methuen Children's Books, London (reproduced with permission).

Theme/ Key value

Courage

Striving for personal development

Title

Emotional courage

Summary

This assembly uses the story of Christopher Reeve to exemplify the kind of personal courage which fights despair and pain, and leads to personal development. It aims to encourage students to find courage in their own lives to face crisies and set-backs.

Resources

Supplied OHT image (p132). Two students to read the news items.

REFLECTION

■ *Show supplied OHT image throughout.*

We start today with a news item from some time ago. It's dated June 1st 1995 and refers to an incident which happened a few days earlier.

Reader 1: *Superman* star Christopher Reeve is paralysed and cannot breathe on his own after breaking his neck in a riding accident, his surgeon said on Wednesday. The doctor refused to speculate on Reeve's chance of recovery.

The actor's headlong fall during a weekend horse-riding accident in Culpeper, Virginia, caused multiple fractures to his first and second cervical vertebrae and also damaged his spinal cord, said Dr. John Jane, a University of Virginia neurosurgeon. Reeve, 42, may require surgery soon to stabilize his upper spine, the doctor said.

Before his appalling accident, Christopher Reeve led an enviable life. He seemed to have it all – brains, good looks, star status, beautiful wife, loving family. What's more, he didn't seem to have struggled to get it all. His mum was a journalist and his dad was a University professor, and even while he was still at his prestigious private school Christopher was appearing on the professional stage. He continued to act professionally while he did a degree in Music and English at university.

So Reeve's success seemed guaranteed even before he landed the title role in the first of the four *Superman* films that were to make him a household name. He was fit and strong too, and loved physical activity. He did all his own stunt work in his films, and enjoyed sailing, flying and horse-riding. Life was good – very good. Then came the news that stunned his fans.

The medics described Reeve's injuries to the press.

Reader 2: 'The fall caused multiple fractures of the first and second cervical vertebrae in his spinal column, a grievous injury that has left the actor paralysed, unable to use any of his limbs or even to breathe without the aid of a respirator.'

No-one can imagine exactly what Christopher Reeve felt when he realised what the fall from his horse had done to his body and to his life. I can only imagine how I might have responded – perhaps you can imagine what you might have felt. You need a lot of support and help to find the courage to face a life changed for ever.

Certainly, no-one could be envious of Christopher Reeve in the days after his accident. Many people hearing about him would look at their own lives and count their blessings. What good are fame and fortune if the rest of your life has to be spent on a respirator and in a wheelchair?

It would not have been surprising if Christopher Reeve had succumbed to self-pity and despair in the face of such a future. And if he had, he would probably have hidden himself away and we would have heard very little about him again.

But in fact, there have been many press reports about Christopher Reeve since his accident and they show a very different picture. Listen to these summaries of some of them:

 ISBN 1 874050 39 2

Reader 1: July 31st 1995: Christopher Reeve is still using a respirator, but can speak clearly and is able to use a powered wheelchair.

Reader 2: December 13th 1995: Reeve leaves hospital. He can manage to breathe for fifteen minutes without the respirator.

Reader 1: January 10th 1996: Reeve becomes co-founder of the Reeve-Irvine Research Centre, dedicated to spinal cord research. Reeve now breathing a full hour without the respirator.

Reader 2: February 21st 1996: Christopher Reeve appears on the Larry King chat-show on American TV. He can now breathe for an hour and a half without the respirator. He speaks about his work with the American Paralysis Association. He has signed a contract to write a book.

Reader 1: March 10th 1996: Reeve appears at the opening of a new rehabilitation centre and says, 'Now we stand on the threshold of full recovery. It can happen. The scientists are ready, willing and able. With support, they will do it.'

Reader 2: May 15th 1996: Reeve meets President Clinton and lobbies the US government for greater funding for spinal research. He says he believes that with funding he could be walking in seven years.

Reader 1: May 27th 1996: Reeve is reported to be planning to direct a new TV film.

Reader 2: June 10th 1996: Christopher Reeve has been asked to direct a stage play. He can now breathe for two and a half hours without the respirator.

Reader 1: July 12th 1996: Reeve takes part in a sailing competition for people with spinal cord injuries.

Reader 2: August 15th 1996: Reeve hosts the Paralympics Opening Ceremony in Atlanta, Georgia. He has recovered some feeling in his spine and left leg and using a tilt table he can stand for long periods at a time.

Reader 1: August 26th 1996: Christopher Reeve addresses the Democratic Party Convention in a full-length speech that includes the following – 'One of the smartest things we can do about disability is to invest in research that will protect us from diseases and lead to cures. This country already has a long history of doing it. When we put our minds to a problem, we find solutions. But our scientists can do more. We have got to give them the chance. And that means more funding for research… We are on the way to getting millions of people around the world like me, up and out of these wheelchairs.'

■ *Thank the readers and dismiss them.*

When that happens, it will be due in no small part to the amazing courage of Christopher Reeve – Superman. *(Pause)*

RESPONSE

Expressions of thankfulness

Let's be grateful that we have our health and we haven't suffered in the way experienced by Christopher Reeve. Let's use his story to help us maintain a sense of perspective about our own situations.

Commitment

Christopher Reeve had already shown great physical courage in his life, and he's continuing to show that in his daily fight to walk again. But what he is also showing now is tremendous emotional courage in his determination to use his future positively. We can all hope – and perhaps pray too – that we never suffer the kind of setback that devastated Christopher Reeve's life. But you will have set-backs, sometimes real crises in your own lives. I hope you will make a decision to face these with the same kind of courage that he has – the courage to climb out of self-pity and despair in order to do something positive and worthwhile. *(Pause)*

Extra Resources

Information taken from original webpage by A.J. Gould is now transferred to webpage by Steven Younis, address http://www.dot.net.au/~younis/reeve/reeve/html See also an article in the August 16 1996 issue of *Time* magazine.

Theme/ Key value

Courage

Striving for personal development

Title

Physical courage

Summary

This assembly explores the values that underlie those working in the rescue services and asks students to consider their own attitudes towards physical courage and selflessness.

Resources

There are no resources needed for this assembly.

REFLECTION

Come with me in your imagination to watch some people at work. It's night-time – well, early hours of the morning in fact. The workplace is a two-storey brick building with enormous ground floor shutters and a large yard or car park that fronts on to the street without a wall. There are lights in the upstairs windows. This is where the workers are. Two men are playing table tennis. Four more are playing cards. A woman sits in an armchair, half-reading a magazine while she chats to another woman who's half-watching a satellite channel on the TV.

Perhaps you've guessed what job they do. Or perhaps you're thinking that whatever it is, it sounds like a cushy number that you wouldn't mind doing yourself.

But suddenly there's a howling alarm. The workers run from where they are and jump through a gap in the floor, grabbing a pole that lands them at ground level. They snatch coats and helmets from racks on the wall and spring into a waiting vehicle.

These men and women are fire-fighters on night-shift, ready at a second's notice to tackle fires of all kinds, mop up dangerous chemical spillages, cut into crashed cars to free trapped occupants, and deal with a host of other dangerous situations.

This time it's a house fire. Breathing apparatus is required – old foam-filled furniture belches out highly toxic smoke. It's a small terraced house and the ground floor is burning fiercely. An ambulance approaches from the other end of the street. The owners of the burning house are being restrained as they scream frantically that their children are upstairs.

Their team leader gives brief instructions and while some of them mobilise the waterhoses, two others make their way into the smoke-filled house. A little light penetrates the entrance hall from the lamps outside. The fire is centred on the main living room, but its doorway is well alight and so is the top of the staircase. Through her sealed helmet, Carla can just see the plastic lampshade on the hall ceiling bending and warping in the heat before the choking black smoke obliterates it from view.

Trusting their suits to protect them, Carla and Gary feel their way through the flames up the stairs to the landing, then split up to search the bedrooms. Carla's working blind now, the smoke is so thick, but at least her helmet allows her to breathe clear oxygen. She knows too well how it will be for the trapped children. If they haven't woken up in the commotion, their lungs will fill with the toxic poison and they will quickly drift from sleep to coma, then death. Speed is vital.

If they've woken, panic will have driven them into a short and hopeless search for air and the smoke claims them fast. It poisons their lungs and blackens their faces. For Carla each new encounter is as heart-wrenching as the first.

Her foot touches something soft. She reaches down, and with a well-trained lift and swing gets an unconscious child on to her shoulder. She heads for the window. It's already open and she can see Gary coming up on the hydraulic lift. Down

 ISBN 1 874050 39 2

below, the mother has a crying child in her arms. The other kid must have got to the window on its own. Carla wonders what's happened to Andy. If both the kids are out, he should be with her by now. What's keeping him? She passes the unconscious child to Gary and turns back into the smoke. It's a quick job to establish Andy's not in this front bedroom. Try the landing next, then the room at the back. If she can get to it.

By now the fire is raging through the top of the house. The landing floor is still okay, but for how long?

In the back room there's a bewildering jumble of obstacles. Recognition comes quickly. Floor partly gone. Furniture toppled over. Bunk beds. Wardrobe. TV. Andy, motionless. He doesn't stir. Carla hauls him out from under the wreckage. The telly must have hit him. There's nothing else that heavy.

She's no idea whether the landing floor will hold the weight of both of them as she drags Andy towards the front bedroom. Gary's there, inside the room now, but holding back from adding his own weight to the burning floor beyond its door. Thankfully, they're soon out of the window and back with their colleagues. Andy's conscious now. He'll need to be checked at the hospital. But his only concern is the kids.

'They'll be fine,' he's told. The ambulance crew have revived the toddler. The fire's under control. Carla's soon on board the fire tender wondering if they'll be in time for the film at five o'clock. *(Pause)*

It takes courage to be a fire-fighter like Carla, the kind of pure physical courage that risks personal danger in order to do a difficult job. Other workers have to have a similar courage – police, paramedics, mountain rescue teams, lifeboat crews.

Some of that courage comes from having complete confidence in the training you've had and in your colleagues. Being brave in times of danger is a little easier when you know what do and how to do it. But what do you think makes people join the fire service in the first place?

■ ***Optional*** *Take some responses from students and summarise, making sure to include them in the text which follows.*

There's the buzz, the excitement of the work, although a lot of it is routine. There's the recognition from others that you're doing a worthwhile job. There's also the motivation to do something for others – to give something rather than take. To be a fire-fighter you have to value life and property and have a commitment to saving it. Your belief that these things are important is such that you have the courage to risk your own life for them.

RESPONSE

Thankfulness

We should all be grateful for those in the services like fire, ambulance and air/sea rescue who show real physical courage in their jobs – some of you may wish thank God that they have that courage. *(Pause)*

Commitment

But what about you? What are your attitudes and values when it comes to showing some courage yourself? Carla's courage was remarkable because it was selfless – she deliberately put someone else's needs before her own. Would you have the courage to do that? Would I? *(Pause)* If you saw someone in our school suffering really badly because of bullying, for example, would you have the courage to stand up for them even though you were risking being hurt yourself? *(Pause)*

Do you believe that courage is important?

Extra Resources

Creighton, J (1985) *Fire Fighting in Action: The Modern British Fire Service*. London: Blandford Press. Wallington, N (1987) *'999': The Accident and Crash Rescue Work of the Fire Service*. Devon: David & Charles.

pfp, 61 Gray's Inn Road, London WC1X 8TL ISBN 1 874050 39 2

Theme/ Key value

Courage

Striving for personal development

Title

The courage of belief

Summary

This assembly tries to help students to find the courage to stand by their beliefs, whatever they may be and in spite of what others around may say.

Resources

There are no resources needed for this assembly.

REFLECTION

It was just a local football match on a field in the recreation grounds, but the supporters lined up on either side of the pitch were loud and exuberant in their encouragement of their players – and in their criticism of the Ref! When the home side scored and their supporters cheered, all the spectators on the other side of the pitch groaned. Except for one small voice that shouted a delighted 'Yes!' A boy aged about nine years old had for some unknown reason got himself fairly and squarely in the middle of the opposition crowd. As he cheered the home side's goal, some of the away supporters rounded on him aggressively.

'Hey – what do you think you're doing?'

'Get out of the way – you should be over there!'

'Shut your face or I'll shut it for you!'

But one of the away supporters – an older man – turned on the others and said, 'Leave him alone. How many of you would cheer that loud if you were the only supporter in the wrong crowd? The kid's got a lot of bottle to yell for his team like that. You keep cheering, son!'

As the man said, it takes a lot of bottle to cheer for your team when you're in the wrong crowd.

It takes a lot of courage to stand up for something you really believe in, especially when you're with people who don't share your views.

Christians remind themselves of this when they think of the story of Peter. He was a fisherman and a close friend of Jesus of Nazareth, and he would be the first to sympathise with anyone in that position.

When Jesus was arrested in Jerusalem, the city was under Roman occupation, so the Jewish authorities who wanted to be rid of Jesus persuaded the Roman authorities that he was trying to topple Roman rule. They knew that the sentence for such an offence was death – execution by crucifixion. To be known as a friend of Jesus was to risk the same death.

Despite this, Peter tried to stay as close as possible when Jesus was taken to the High Priest's house for questioning. There were lots of people in the courtyard warming themselves at an open fire, but when one of them recognised him as a friend of Jesus, Peter lost his bottle.

Here's how the Christian Bible tells it:

❝Peter was still down in the courtyard when one of the High Priest's servant-girls came by. When she saw Peter warming himself, she looked straight at him and said, 'You, too, were with Jesus of Nazareth.'

But he denied it. 'I don't know... I don't understand what you are talking about,' he answered, and went out into the passage. Just then a cockerel crowed.

The servant-girl saw him there and began to repeat to the bystanders, 'He is one of them!' But Peter denied it again.

A little while later the bystanders accused Peter again, 'You can't deny that you are one of them, because you, too, are from Galilee.'

 ISBN 1 874050 39 2

Then Peter said, 'I swear that I am telling the truth! May God punish me if I am not! I do not know the man you are talking about!'

Just then a cockerel crowed a second time, and Peter remembered how Jesus had said to him, 'Before the cock crows twice, you will say three times that you do not know me.' And he broke down and cried."

Faced with the fear of dying a horrible death, Peter couldn't stand by his convictions. He just didn't have it in him. At least not at that stage.

But just a few weeks later, Peter was in the centre of Jerusalem, standing on a balcony and preaching as loud as he could about Jesus to the hundreds of visiting Jews who had travelled there for a huge festival. The Romans were still in power. The Jewish authorities had seen Jesus executed as they'd planned, and they were determined to have anyone preaching about him executed in the same way. But this time, Peter has no qualms about being recognised as a friend of Jesus.

He talked about Jesus performing miracles and showing his divine nature. He told the crowd how they'd allowed sinful men to kill Jesus and how he'd overcome death and was still alive. Peter stood up and spoke loudly and clearly about his beliefs.

It's as if Peter has had a 'make-over' like you sometimes see in a magazine, where they have two pictures of the same person, 'before' and 'after' they've had the glamour treatment. Something has happened to them between picture one and picture two and you can hardly believe it's the same person.

Something must have happened to Peter between picture one and picture two. You can hardly believe it's the same person.

The Christian Bible tells us that Peter really believed that God had raised Jesus from the dead to prove that he was who he said he was. It says that Peter and his friends met the risen Jesus several times and that Jesus forgave Peter for denying him. Peter also believed that the power of God which had raised Jesus to life was available to all believers to help them preach about Jesus.

To have the courage to engage openly in an activity that puts you at risk of being arrested and executed, you have to really believe in something. It was what Peter believed about Jesus that gave him the courage to be a Jesus supporter.

RESPONSE

Commitment

Here is a prayer for courage for someone who is trying to stand up for what they believe in. If you're a religious believer, perhaps you might like to make it your own prayer today. If not, you might want to think about these ideas and commit yourself to most of them.

Lord God,
Give me understanding to know what is right,
faithfulness when I'm tempted to deny it,
and courage to stand by what I believe.
If people laugh at my ideas, help me to be patient.
If people laugh at my beliefs, help me to persevere.
Help me to be true to myself, true to my beliefs and true to you.
Amen.

Extra Resources

The Bible extracts are from Mark's gospel Chapter 15 verses 66 to 72. Peter's story can be found in the Acts of the Apostles Chapter 3 verses 22 to 24 and verse 36. *The Good News Bible.*

Theme/ Key value

Courage

Striving for personal development

Title

The courage to be yourself

Summary This assembly focuses on some of the mechanisms required in finding the courage to be yourself. Although recommended for KS4 some schools may find it appropriate at KS3 as well.

Resources There are no resources needed for this assembly.

REFLECTION

■ ***Optional*** *Adapt the following paragraph if you are not using the theme as a whole.*

As you know, in our assemblies recently we've been talking about courage. We've looked at physical courage, emotional courage, moral courage... One of the principal things we need courage for is to be ourselves. You need to know and be comfortable with yourself if you are to achieve your potential – both here at school and when you leave. That may sound like an easy thing to do, but actually it's not – it takes great courage. That courage gives you determination and helps you to realise and stand up for the things that you value and believe in.

Today's story is based on the true experiences of a young person like you, and it may ring some bells...

❝The year tens were back in school after doing their Work Experience and the stories were flowing thick and fast. Everyone had their turn, so eventually it came round to Damon.

'Hey, Damon!,' someone shouted. 'How did you get on at Holden's Haulage?'

Damon gave his usual broad grin and shrugged. 'Well, of course the coffee machine waited to go wrong till I turned up and pressed the button. Ever tried getting forty litres of hot coffee into a small plastic cup?'

You were never sure with Damon how much he was exaggerating, but he always made people laugh. However, while he laughed along with his friends, inside Damon was worried. He had one question that was currently occupying most of his waking moments. What was he going to do after his GCSEs?

His best subjects were English and History. It would be easy just to drift into the Sixth Form and do the A-levels. But he knew that the expected route then would be university and he wasn't sure that was what he wanted. His parents were okay – they didn't pressure him the way some did. But the teachers were harder to persuade. He knew they saw it as a waste of a good student, someone who could get into university but didn't want to.

He got round that by pointing out that he was actually quite good at Design and Technology. So the teachers suggested engineering. That ruled out university because he'd never get the necessary A-level maths even if by some miracle he got a good grade in GCSE.

What Damon actually like doing best was hospital radio. He was at the County General most evenings and weekends, even if he wasn't actually doing a show. He liked going round the wards, talking to the patients and getting their requests. Especially the kids' ward. He loved larking around with them. Then, when he was the duty disc jockey, he'd visualise the kids he'd met and talk directly to them through his microphone. But hospital radio is voluntary. If only you could get paid for making kids laugh!

Because of this, Damon had asked to be sent to the local radio station on Work Experience to see what you had to do to get into professional broadcasting. But because the teachers all knew Damon was a bit of a clown they thought he was just looking for a scam, so they sent him instead to Holden's Haulage to get some insight into heavy vehicle maintenance.

One coffee break, there he was talking about what he did at the hospital, when one of the mechanics said, 'I did my apprenticeship

pfp, 61 Gray's Inn Road, London WC1X 8TL ISBN 1 874050 39 2

opposite the General, at Adkins Engineering Works. It's a four-year hands-on course with day release, but they only take ten apprentices a year, so you have to be good.'

Suddenly Damon had found the ideal solution – engineering by day and hospital radio in the evenings. So, he put 110% effort into his various D and T projects, got good grades in his GCSEs and eventually won a coveted apprenticeship at the engineering works.

But still Damon wished he could get just a taste of professional broadcasting. In the small amount of spare time he had he also wrote regularly to the local radio station, sending them tapes of his hospital programmes in the hope of being taken on as a volunteer. After two years and many letters and tapes they finally responded. He was invited in as a weekend helper, doing little jobs for the professional broadcasters and seeing how they went about their work.

At the end of his four-year apprenticeship Damon found himself facing another difficult decision. The engineering firm offered him a permanent job – but he didn't want it. His workmates couldn't understand why not, just as some of his teachers never understood why he hadn't wanted to go to university.

But by now the local radio station manager had seen how keen Damon was to become a broadcaster. He'd also seen how faithful he was to his engineering apprenticeship. Damon might be a clown, but if he said he was going to do something, he did it, even if it was a four-year commitment. It was a pretty mature attitude, which impressed the manager. He offered Damon the chance to prove himself as a broadcaster, doing interviews and outside broadcasts. He'd only be paid for each individual job, which some weeks wouldn't add up to much at all.

His parents said if he wanted to give it a go they'd support him for a year, but they wouldn't be able to afford it after that. They needn't have worried. At the end of the year, Damon had his own daily show and as much extra work as he could handle.

But the memories of the fun he'd had with the youngsters on the kids' ward stayed with Damon. Once again he started writing letters, this time looking for work in children's television. It took a long time and a lot of patience. He sent sample video 'show-reels' to nearly 200 TV companies before he was taken on by one of the major terrestrials.”

Well – what do you think happened? As you might have guessed, Damon's persistence paid off. I'm not going to tell you his real name, but he's now a popular presenter on national television. (Don't forget – this is a true story.) He had a lot of luck and support in getting there, but as we've seen, it also took a lot of personal courage.

RESPONSE

Commitment

Side-stepping the pressure to go to university, proving that he wasn't just wasting his talents, and knuckling down to the apprenticeship that taught him skills that would be useful if his dreams all failed – all that took some courage.

Writing letters for two years to the radio station, then circulating 200 TV companies – that took perseverance and patience. In a way, that's courage.

At each turning point, Damon needed the courage to think hard about which was the most appropriate decision for him, for the kind of person he was, the kind of person he wanted to become. He needed the courage to think through the reasons for his decisions each time, so that he was ready with a good answer for those who questioned his decision.

This is a very special kind of courage. It helps you to achieve your dreams. It's called 'the courage to be yourself'.

You're making decisions now about your future. Think about them carefully. Have the courage to think about who you are and what you want. And let that courage help you towards your aim. (Pause)

© pfp 1998 ISBN 1 874050 39 2

The Secondary Assembly File

Just think how long it takes you to put together a meaningful assembly that fits into your Collective Worship policy. **The Secondary Assembly File** helps you provide thought-provoking, attention-grabbing material for a fraction of what your time is worth.

And **The Secondary Assembly File** will help you meet Ofsted's requirements for Collective Worship.

Subscribers to **The Secondary Assembly File** receive

1 A total of **90** brand new assemblies on 18 key themes, well-written and carefully researched, saving you precious time

2 assemblies which incorporate a response about a range of personal, social, moral and spiritual issues

3 differentiated assemblies for younger and older secondary students, and sixth formers (many of the sixth form assemblies are suitable for 15 and 16 year olds)

4 a free 70+ minute CD of appropriate assembly music

5 free OHT masters

6 a free hard-wearing ring-binder.

And all the material is **fully photocopiable** for use within your school.

The assemblies are written by a team of writers, all of whom deliver assemblies in secondary schools, and have a finger on the pulse of what interests and captivates a young audience. Our editor, Larry Hartley, is a deputy headteacher in a large comprehensive. Along with our writing team, Larry ensures that the assemblies are broadly Christian, and of a spiritual nature, while clearly recognising our multifaith society. These assemblies are designed to develop individual thinking and, most importantly, to allow you to express your school's values.

If you order the current series of **The Secondary Assembly File** you will receive it on continuous subscription. Once you have sent in your first order, you don't have to do anything else. Unless you tell us otherwise you will receive an issue of the file you have ordered each term, although, of course, you can cancel at any time if you so wish – we send you a reminder in the final issue of each series.

The first issue of each file comes with a hard-wearing ring-binder. All the pages are loose-leaf and hole-punched, and completely photocopiable within the purchasing institution.